SELINA ELISON

BULIMIA

Understanding the Voice Inside My Daughter's Head

First published by Berlu Books 2024

Copyright © 2024 by Selina Elison

All rights reserved. No part of this publication may be reproduced, stored or transmitted in any form or by any means, electronic, mechanical, photocopying, recording, scanning, or otherwise without written permission from the publisher. It is illegal to copy this book, post it to a website, or distribute it by any other means without permission.

Selina Elison asserts the moral right to be identified as the author of this work.

Although the author has made every effort to ensure that the information in this book was correct at press time, and while this book is designed to provide accurate information in regard to the subject covered, the author assumes no responsibility for errors, inaccuracies, omissions, or any other inconsistencies. This book is meant as a valuable source of information for the reader, however, it is not meant as a substitute for direct expert advice. If such level of advice is required, the services of a competent professional should be sought.

The names and identifying characteristics of certain individuals have been changed to protect their privacy.

www.selinaelison.com/ Instagram @selinaelison_writer

Edited by Sage Taylor Kingsley/ www.SageforYourPage.com

Cover photograph © Shutterstock

Te Puna Mātauranga o Aotearoa/National Library of New Zealand

First edition

ISBN: 978-0-47-369786-0

This book was professionally typeset on Reedsy.
Find out more at reedsy.com

What matters in life is not what happens to you but what you remember – and how you remember it.

                                        Gabriel García Marquéz

Preface

Bulimia nervosa is nobody's fault. It is a multifactorial mental illness. Anyone of any age can suffer from it. Because it is a relatively new eating disorder in the history of mental illness, parents or partners who care for a loved one with bulimia may discover that healthcare professionals or family members and friends possess only limited knowledge about it. They will meet people who still believe that suffering from bulimia is a choice, that it is the parent's fault, that anorexia is the only serious eating disorder, and/or that people with bulimia, who don't look emaciated, are not sick enough to deserve treatment. Initially, the carers themselves also may share some of these beliefs, consciously or unconsciously.

I won't exclude myself here. When my daughter was diagnosed with bulimia, I knew nothing about this eating disorder. But ignorance is always dangerous. In the case of bulimia, it allows the red-flag behaviours of those who suffer from this serious illness to go unnoticed, sometimes for years.

Parents and partners of bulimia patients should be, and in most cases are, highly concerned and prepared to do anything to help their loved one. Compassionate support is a crucial component of recovery, but the impacts that bulimia has on people's physical and emotional health, their romantic relationship, and their employment and finances, are huge and often underestimated.

I wrote this memoir to shine a light on the lonely and frightening reality of those who look after their loved one through the recovery process. I deeply feel they deserve greater understanding and better support from healthcare providers, friends, extended family, and society in general.

Most importantly, however, I wish to connect on a personal level with those who navigate this difficult situation.

As on any journey, we make mistakes. I truly hope that you will learn from mine. I also hope to show you how practical strategies for recovery can work in a real-life situation. And finally, I hope that you will find solace and encouragement for yourself in my story. Cut yourself some slack, look after your own well-being, and remember, we can only do our best. One step at a time.

Acknowledgements

This book would not exist without the trust, kindness, generosity, and courage of my daughter. I thank you wholeheartedly for giving me permission to write about your recovery journey. I love you very much.

Many other people contributed to the development of the book.

I am particularly grateful to my friend, Kirsty McGill, and to my mentor, Casey Eileen. You were the ones who inspired me to write this memoir. Thank you.

Big thanks go to Sage Taylor Kingsley for copyediting and proofreading. To my amazing partner, Johnny Martin, for reading my first draft and encouraging me to keep going. To Matt Klimczak, Simona Moroni, and Bree Hudson for reading my final draft and offering detailed feedback.

Thank you to my spiritual teacher, Robina Courtin, whose teachings keep me grounded in life.

While I wrote this memoir, I travelled. Thank you to all of you fellow travellers who listened to my story and shared with me your knowledge about and experience with eating disorders. A special thank you to Sam Thureau and Eva Pissavini from France. You made me believe in the importance of this book.

Finally, thank you to all my family and friends for your loving support.

Chapter 1

My conversation with Venerable Sara felt absurd at the time. But her words kept coming back to me over the next two and a half years, although I lacked the courage to understand their true meaning. I can see this now.

Ten weeks had passed since my sixteen-year-old daughter, Fiona, had been diagnosed with *bulimia nervosa*. I was attending a three-day retreat at a Buddhist centre, not far from the town where I live in New Zealand. During one of the morning sessions, the teaching nun invited us to talk about anything weighing on our minds. After much hesitation, I spoke. Ven. Sara tipped her head while she listened closely to my story.

I confessed my anguish of being unable to find adequate support for Fiona.

"I'm at my wits end. And I'm worried sick." My body tensed as I heard my own words echo through the meditation hall.

"You could stop worrying," the nun suggested, her gentle eyes fixed on me with a genuine curiosity.

"That's impossible!" I burst out, my hands trembling. "What if she dies?"

"Well, let's imagine you actually stopped worrying, what do you think would happen?"

"Nothing," I said, without knowing what I meant by that and if it was the right answer.

"So, why do you worry?"

"Because I love her," my voice quivered. *Don't cry, Selena. Don't cry. Nobody cries here.* "I want her to be happy again. To smile. I'd feel guilty if I didn't worry."

"Guilt is a Western thing," she said warmly.

Bewildered, I looked down on my legs. Crossed in a perfect lotus position, they gave the impression that I was coping just fine. I closed my eyes. It was easier to suppress my tears this way. Behind me, someone coughed, muffled into a scarf. A heavy silence followed, which seemed to rest entirely on my shoulders.

Finally, Ven. Sara continued to teach.

Half listening, I examined her. She had a beautiful Dutch face with blue eyes that appeared bigger than they were because her head was shaved. Burgundy robes wrapped around her soft body. *She must be in her forties,* I thought, *roughly ten years younger than me.* Her voice was kind, but her words stoic. I could tell that she wasn't going to take pity on me.

But I longed for someone to sympathise with me. To tell me that I didn't deserve this. I had embraced motherhood with such noble intentions and zeal. Now the bubble had burst, and everything seemed so wrong.

"We must learn to accept reality," she'd said earlier.

Only a nun would talk like that. A nun who wasn't a mother.

Three months prior, exactly one year after my brother's death, I had travelled to Germany to visit my mother in her tidy city apartment. Things were different now with my brother gone. Sadness had crushed my mother, and she had stopped talking to old friends. Her eyes were tearing all the time from a year of crying. The waiting in between my visits had become wearisome for her, and the distance between New Zealand and Germany had grown.

I had arrived in Munich, the city where I had grown up, with the intention of lifting the veil of her loneliness, at least for a few weeks. Blessed with unfailing sunshine, I took her on long, interesting walks that we complemented with hours of people-watching in restaurants with outdoor tables and blankets. I showed her photos of Fiona and Eric. We laughed again. I felt content and reassured that by the end of my stay, I would leave her in a better space than the year before.

"I don't envy you. I couldn't do this long trip anymore." My mother's head was peeking around my bedroom door.

"I don't mind it. I can sleep on the plane. Better than having to go to work."

CHAPTER 1

I snickered.

"Will you fit everything in?"

"Easy," I said as I jammed the last packing cube into my travel bag, zipped it closed, and gave the bag a quick pat. "Voilà! Got everything. Ready to go!"

My phone buzzed. I glanced at the screen. It was Fiona's high school. *Bizarre*, I thought, *I hope she hasn't had an accident.* My stomach tightened. I rushed into the living room to sit down on the sofa before picking up.

A female voice introduced herself as Jane Paladino. I was familiar with her face. I'd seen her in the staff room and knew she was the school's councillor, but I'd never spoken to her. She came straight to the point. This morning, Anthony, my daughter's boyfriend, had brought a tearful Fiona into her office. At first Fiona had refused to open her mouth, but eventually she had disclosed that she had been throwing up her food for the last ten months. Basically, she was suffering from what you'd call bulimia, Jane explained.

"Where is she now?" I stuttered.

"Here with me in my office." She paused. "I told her that I'm not allowed to keep this confidential. She's underage, you see. You need to know."

Apparently, Fiona had pleaded with her not to call her father.

"She's feeling terribly anxious," Jane continued. "But I reassured her that you'll be understanding."

"Of course."

Then she asked me if I knew what bulimia was. I said yes, because I didn't want her to think that I was uneducated and ignorant on top of clueless about my daughter's well-being. Jane asked further who was responsible for looking after Fiona. Her older brother? I nodded, forgetting that she couldn't see me.

Jane didn't wait for my answer. She promised to check on Fiona every morning before her first lesson and during lunchtime until I was home.

"But that's all I can do." She sounded resolute.

I understood. *She doesn't want to be blamed in case anything happens.* "Thank you."

There was a long pause. I was burning to know details, reasons, phew.... I took a few shaky breaths, but I didn't dare ask. *Fiona is probably listening to the call.* I could sense that Jane wanted to keep the conversation short.

"Ten months?" I stammered. "You said ten months?"

"Yes."

"My flight leaves tomorrow. It's a two-day trip, which means I won't be in the country until Wednesday. I can come and see you with Fiona on Thursday morning first thing. Is that okay?"

"Sounds good," she said and then she asked me if I was all right.

"Erm ... it's a shock. But yes, I'm fine," I responded. I thanked Jane for calling me.

She wished me a safe trip and hung up.

My phone slid out of my hand and dropped into my lap.

"Is everything okay?"

My mother had been watching me from a chair across the room. I cleared my throat.

"Yes, everything is good."

"I'm glad," she said. "What shall we have for dinner, then? It's your last night."

"Anything, *Mutti*, anything will do."

We got up. My mother walked into the kitchen, and I walked into the bathroom. I switched the ceiling light on, locked the door, and let my body sink on the closed toilet lid. My limbs suddenly hurt as if battered from a street fight. I bent forwards and grabbed my stomach although I didn't feel sick. I felt cold.

I stared at the oval-shaped bathmat in front of my feet. *It must be at least thirty years old*, I thought. Its colour had faded. I looked up. The blue grout between the white wall tiles had faded, too. Two towels hung on the wall next to the sink. Above one of the towels, there was a sticky label with my name on it. My mother always labelled the towels so that we wouldn't use hers by accident.

Every time Fiona had come to Munich, she'd be amused about her grandma's peculiar ways of doing things. "*Oma* is such a crack up," she'd say to me and snicker.

The last time I had sat on the toilet lid had been on the day of my brother's funeral, but it had been six o'clock in the morning then. Cautiously I'd snuck

CHAPTER 1

out of the bedroom where Fiona and I slept, my hands holding on to a piece of paper with the eulogy speech that I'd written on the plane. I would be the only one speaking at his funeral that day and I'd decided that I would be like steel. I would speak clearly and without a trembling in my voice because I feared that my eighty-seven-year-old mother would collapse if I started to cry. I remembered the funeral now because for months afterwards, I had worn this shatterproof brave face.

I am good at hiding my sorrows. I can do it again, I told myself

Bulimia, the councillor had said. *Well, what on Earth is the difference between anorexia and bulimia?* The only person who I'd ever known throwing up her food was the anorexic girl in my high-school class, the one with the freckles. Everybody had bullied her because she was the teacher's pet and her parents were gay. She ended up looking like a stick insect. One day I saw a huge clump of her hair fall out. Fiona hadn't lost any weight nor clumps of hair. So maybe that was the difference.

I rested my head on my hands and shut my eyes, picturing Fiona next to me on a pier in the Marlborough Sounds, hoping to spot a dolphin. Her relaxed body feeling heavy and warm against mine. Her joyful voice chattering away about all the naughty things that her friends had been up to, but their parents didn't know anything about. I'd considered myself lucky then. She'd always told me everything. It had seemed as if we had had a special bond.

So, why, for heaven's sake, did she start this throwing up business? What's upsetting her so much? And why hasn't she said anything? Doesn't she trust me anymore? Ten months. How could I not have noticed?

My mother called. Dinner was ready. I joined her at the kitchen table, forcing myself to act nonchalant.

"I'll miss the bread," I said grabbing a slice of sourdough. "Maybe I should start making my own."

"I hope the kids have coped. You've been away for such a long time." She obviously wasn't listening.

"*Mutti*, they aren't kids anymore. Eric is twenty-two and Fiona sixteen."

"You know what I mean. They'll be happy to have you back."

"Tom drove home every weekend to be with them."

"Still, I hope they ate well during the week."

"They know how to cook."

"I miss them both. Fiona is such a fine girl, so well-educated and kind."

"I know."

Had I been in my own home, I would have researched bulimia right then and spent the whole night reading, but my mother didn't have the Internet. For the short amount of time that I was in Munich, I hadn't bothered getting a German sim card. For an instant, I'd contemplated buying roaming data, but then I decided against it. I owed it to my mother to be present. I only ever managed to visit her for three weeks out of the year. Together we cleaned the kitchen, then we watched the evening news and at a quarter past eight her favourite show: *Let's Dance*.

"Remember, the last time you were here, we watched this show with Fiona," my mother said. "She is such a talented ballet dancer. Does she still dance?"

"She stopped. Just recently."

"What a shame."

"She goes to the gym now."

I rubbed the skin of my hands until it began to hurt. I was nervous and frightened. What if something happened to her before I'd arrive? Hopefully, she'd be smart enough to sleep at her boyfriend's for the next two nights while I would be on planes.

She can tell her father eventually, in her own time, Jane had said. In an ideal world, I would have respected Fiona's wishes. But during the car ride from the airport to my husband's stuffy Christchurch hotel room, I decided to tell Tom everything I knew. I had to give him a reason why I was rushing home instead of staying with him for the night.

"Fiona doesn't want you to know just yet, because she feels ashamed," I said.

We were sitting on his bed, the only piece of furniture in the room we could sit on. Tom had rented the room for the year that his company had asked him to work away from home. I looked at him. His face had turned pallid. His dark brown eyes were watery. He was quite the sensitive one, and I could see this

CHAPTER 1

was too much for him to digest. I took his hands to comfort him and lowered my eyes, so he wouldn't see my own distress.

"I should quit my job and come home," he suggested. *Typical. Any excuse to get out of his job. The last thing we need right now is financial difficulties.* Not that we were poor, but I hadn't been able to get a full-time teaching position since we had moved out of Christchurch and farther up the coast. My relief teaching income wasn't reliable.

"No, absolutely not," I snapped to stomp out his foolish idea. "What are *you* going to do anyway? We don't know how to cure bulimia. We need to get professional help, and besides, you hardly have three months left in the city."

He nodded and then twisted his neck as if it were sore.

"I'll try to convince Fiona that she needs to talk to you when you'll be home Friday night. I'll tell her that you need to know, regardless."

He nodded again.

"I ought to go now, darling," I said looking at my watch.

While Tom walked me to the bus station, he mentioned a colleague in Wellington. Her daughter had struggled with bulimia.

"They hired a nutritionist to sort out meals, and the girl was fine in no time," he said to make us both feel better. I didn't believe him. God knows why, but I had this weird idea in my head that it would take at least a year for Fiona to be back to normal.

Although it was dark when the bus pulled into town, I saw them immediately. Fiona stood wrapped up in Anthony's strong arms, and behind them was Eric. The dark circles that had formed beneath Fiona's eyes were visible from the distance. Her long hair was stringy as if it hadn't been washed in days. She looked exhausted, but she smiled as soon as she saw me wave. I quickly hopped off the bus.

"Mummy, I've missed you so much."

"I've missed you, too, Poppy," I said and opened my arms. I embraced her warmly and gave her a kiss on the cheek. Before I turned to hug the boys, I squeezed her a tad tighter, shaking slightly.

Anthony went to retrieve my bag from the luggage compartment of the bus, then we jumped into Eric's beat-up Toyota and drove home.

With the little bit of energy that I had left, I made cups of tea for everybody, totally forgetting that Anthony disliked hot drinks.

"You've been away for too long," he laughed. "Hockey players don't drink that stuff."

Instead, he helped himself to a glass of water, several slices of bread, and some leftover chicken. For a while, we stood in the kitchen and chitchatted about Oma, Germany, and the upcoming school exams. Eric picked up Fuzzy, our cat, and held her right in front of my face, like he always did when he ran out of things to say. I took the cat off him and signalled that I needed sleep.

"Good you're back, Mum," he said and tapped me on the shoulder. "Good night, everyone."

"Night, Eric," Fiona and Anthony harped in unison.

I quickly pulled a bag of apple lollies out of my hand luggage and pressed it into Eric's hand. They were his favourite. With a big grin, he shuffled downstairs to his ground-floor apartment.

I whizzed around the house, switched all the bright lights off, and then I crumbled into the dark green velvet armchair in the lounge area, worn out from the trip and the tension. Fiona and Anthony took seats across from me on the grey sofa. I pulled the chair forward so our knees would touch. For a few minutes, we looked at each other in intimate silence, unsure of what to say.

"I'm so grateful that you spoke to Mrs. Paladino," I whispered.

Tears began to roll down my daughter's swollen face, dripping quietly from her chin into her lap. Her beautiful green eyes looked at me, scared.

Anthony put his arm around her, and she leaned her head on his shoulder.

I stroked her knees and gathered my thoughts. Even though I'd been on a fifty-hour journey with more than enough time to think, I still didn't know whether what I was going to say to Fiona tonight would upset her or not. *How am I supposed to prepare myself for a bulimia conversation when I know nothing about it?*

"I'm so happy to be back home, Poppy. I can help you now. You're not alone with this anymore." I paused and reached for her hand. "How did it start,

CHAPTER 1

darling? What's been going on? Tell me."

Fiona's tears were unstoppable now. She buried her face in Anthony's chest. Anthony and I sat motionless. When our eyes met, I hoped he wouldn't see my uneasiness. He looked concerned. I smiled softly at him ... and waited.

At last, she lifted her head and spoke.

Since the beginning of the school year, she said, she'd stopped eating her packed lunches in front of the boys in her year group. She'd thrown them in the garbage because the boys had convinced her that her legs were too fat. "Eating again, are you? With those legs? " they'd said.

So, she had put herself on a strict diet. Each day she would come home from school or sports starving, but she would wait out until dinner, only to serve herself a little bit of whatever I'd cooked, the smallest amount she could get away with.

"You always watched how much I ate and nagged me about eating more. You said I needed energy because I was still growing."

I nodded. Yes, I remembered being concerned, but Fiona hadn't been losing weight, in fact, at some stage I'd even thought she'd gained a few pounds. And I had believed her when she'd claimed that she had already eaten something at a friend's place. Once a week she would skip dinner altogether.

She said she would ignore her hunger for days, watching her stomach constrict. Not to mention that every day she would go to the gym or on runs, begging for her legs to get thinner, not just to keep fit. Then, out of nowhere, hunger would hit her hard, forcing her to break down and binge on bowls of cereal or cookies or other snack food; whatever she could find in the pantry, really, because her body demanded it. Disappointed in herself for not sticking to her diet, she would stick her finger down her throat and get rid of the binged food. With the water running in the shower, nobody would hear her.

Sometimes she'd binge and purge while I'd be in the garden, mowing the lawns or planting.

I felt lightheaded.

My poor child was going through hell while I was happily planting daffodils. I screwed up. It's all my fault.

I rubbed my forehead to wipe away my thoughts and to refocus. I wanted to know how severe her bulimia was and how often she vomited, but I hesitated to ask her, out of respect. Surely, she didn't want Anthony to know, and most likely she didn't want me to know either. I suspected it happened every single day. Actually, I didn't need to hear it.

"Why did you never say anything, sweetheart?"

"Because the one time I threw up in Germany, you were so mad at me."

Embarrassed, I looked away. I remembered the scene vividly.

A few days after my brother's funeral, I'd caught her throwing up, because in my mother's apartment you heard everything.

"Don't you start that!" I had shouted. "It's dangerous. It can kill you."

Stressed from all the other stuff that was going on, I had wanted to scare her, I mean *really* scare her, because subconsciously I feared that she had made herself vomit like I had heard these anorexics did. After all, my dead brother was her favourite uncle. It was a challenging time for all of us.

"No, Mum," she had insisted. "I feel sick. It's Oma's weird cooking."

There was nothing wrong with her grandmother's cooking, but I had preferred to believe her. And just in case she'd lied to me, I'd done my best. I'd warned her.

"I felt fat because I wasn't getting any exercise," Fiona explained.

I also knew, but I didn't want to bring it up in front of Anthony, that shortly after we had returned from Germany, Fiona's previous boyfriend, Marc, had ended their eight-month long relationship without giving her a reason. Just dumped her. Fiona was heartbroken. Marc and she had never argued, therefore she probably thought if only her legs were as thin as those of some of the other girls, she could win him back.

It all added up now.

"I know throwing up is unhealthy."

I was glad she was the one who said it.

"You know," she continued, "Eric was always downstairs playing his video games when you were away, so I binged and threw up as much as I wanted. With each day, it got worse until I lost total control. I slept at Tony's a lot. It felt safer."

Anthony nodded. "Most evenings, she came over to mine. I could tell something was wrong because she always looked so incredibly sad. But when I asked her what's up, she never said anything. She just cried."

Then one night, Anthony had heard her puke. It was the first time she had ever thrown up in someone else's house besides the one time at her grandmother's. Alarmed, he had confronted her. Too worn out to hold back any longer, she had confessed her plight. After hours of talking, they both decided that she should see the school councillor the following morning. But when daylight came, she felt mortified by the thought of having to admit her shameful behaviour to a woman she didn't know.

"I literally had to drag her by her school jacket," Anthony said.

"Lucky you're a strong guy, aye?" I smiled at him, deeply grateful for his care and determination. "How do you know about bulimia?"

"Truthfully, I'm not too sure what it is, but I've heard it's kinda dangerous," he said.

I looked over to Fiona and saw her blushing.

"Let me give you a hug," I said and squeezed next to her. "Listen, I'm so proud of you. Really. I know sometimes it's not easy to ask for help. But you've done the right thing. Now I'll have to do my bit and read up on bulimia to thoroughly understand what's going on and learn how to support you best. Tomorrow we'll go see Mrs. Paladino. Has she been helpful?"

"Yes, she's so nice. She asked me to imagine that the voice in my head belongs to this little guy who sits on my shoulder. Whenever he asks me all these unhealthy things to do, she said, I should argue with him and refuse to follow his orders."

"Interesting," I said and hopped back into the armchair. I looked straight into my daughter's eyes. "Fiona, darling, you're such a good-looking girl. When people bully other people, it's usually to cover up their own insecurities. Don't believe these stupid boys in your year group. Right, Tony?"

Anthony agreed with me, and he gently stroked Fiona's head.

"You have no idea how much we all love you," I said.

Fiona responded with a shy smile.

"Okay," I said and stood up. "I think we need to get some rest."

Anthony rolled himself off the sofa, and Fiona jumped on top of him. Light flirtatious punches flew through the air.

"You've got no chance," he roared.

Fiona shrieked.

"Honestly, guys! Do you always have to wrestle?"

Anthony's energy was too much for me. I slipped out of the lounge to take a shower. When I finally pulled myself upstairs to my bedroom, I heard Fiona giggle. In my ears, it sounded like the onset of rain after a tiresome drought.

Jane Paladino was standing patiently in the doorframe of her office when Fiona and I came rushing down the narrow school corridor to see her. Everything about Jane indicated professional honesty: the beige chino pants, the dark-blue polo shirt, the foot-friendly suede sandals, even the handshake before we sat down. Jane had set up three chairs for us away from her desk.

For most of the meeting, Jane focused entirely on my daughter. She repeatedly advised Fiona to visualise a dwarf on her shoulder as the source of the voice encouraging her to binge and purge.

Why a dwarf? I asked myself. *Shouldn't she be calling it a blimming monster?* Externalising the voice inside her head was helpful, Jane said.

Okay, I got it. Then Jane acknowledged that she didn't know all that much about eating disorders.

"I've made a referral to the Public Mental Health Services. And I've printed out a bunch of help sheets for you to take home, along with the referral to the GP." She concluded our meeting.

Barely an hour later, we sat in Dr. Stevens' clinic. I was glad that the tall fifty-something man could fit us in at such short notice. He was the kind of holistic doctor who actually looked at you while you spoke. I liked that he was approachable, in contrast to those arrogant pricks who assumed rather than listened.

First of all, he praised Fiona for being honest. Then he went through a list of unpleasant standard questions. But he spoke in a kind voice and with a compassionate smile. I sat quietly next to Fiona, silently wishing her strength.

"For how long have you engaged in these behaviours?"

"Not sure," she answered. "I think it really started at the beginning of

CHAPTER 1

January."

"Mm-hmm, okay, and we're in the middle of November now."

As expected, Dr. Stevens diagnosed *bulimia nervosa*.

"It's a complex mental illness. It would be best if you saw a psychologist."

"We have an appointment with the mental health nurses next week," I said.

"Fantastic," he said and proceeded to explain that Fiona's blood had to be tested for electrolyte imbalance, potassium levels, and mineral and glucose deficiencies. Why exactly, he didn't say.

I knew Fiona was deadly afraid of needles because the few times she'd been in hospital, the nurses had struggled with finding her veins and they had ended up stabbing her like you would stab a piece of chicken with a fork. And once she'd fainted while giving blood. I was sure that those horrible scenarios were rewinding in front of Fiona's eyes as she looked at Dr. Stevens in shock.

Affectionately, I put my arm around her shoulders. But her fear also sparked a sense of satisfaction in me. *Maybe from now on she will think twice about vomiting.* I falsely assumed that fear could make her snap out of this eating disorder.

After the doctor's visit, we briefly stopped at the supermarket.

"Why don't you choose some things that you like?" I suggested. "We could make pizza again. Didn't you say Tony was coming over later? He loves those chocolate-chip cookies, doesn't he? Why don't you get some for him and a few treats for yourself?"

Fiona nodded. She turned around, reached for a net with avocados and placed it in the shopping trolley.

I went to pick up a pineapple. When I returned to the trolley, I saw her moving towards me as if she was sleepwalking. Her body had stiffened up, and her skin had turned a greenish white. She looked dazed and ice cold.

I halted in my steps.

"Mummy, I can't be in a supermarket."

Confused, I stared at her.

"It's scary to be around so much food. I can't decide what I want to eat."

My heart began to race as I quickly dropped the pineapple in the shopping cart to free my hands and gently hug her tense body. "Let's run through the store then, Poppy. I only need to pick up a few more items."

Fiona shook her head and demanded the car keys. My eyes followed her as she walked slowly but deliberately out of the supermarket. *What has suddenly happened to my daughter?* She had always gone shopping with me.

I turned my trolley around and nearly hit a girl Fiona's age.

"Oh, sorry," I mumbled and looked at her, but she hadn't even noticed me. She was busy throwing bags of crisps on top of pies, chocolate bars, and all the other junk in her mother's cart. A younger boy in school uniform tried to kick her against the shin while carrying a one-litre bottle of sparkling soft drink under his arm. He missed. Their mother grimaced at both of them.

I firmly clutched the shopping cart handle, lowered my head and rushed past them to stifle the arising envy.

A week later, Emily, a cosily plumb nurse with a motherly face, welcomed Tom, Fiona, and me into the local mental health clinic and asked us to take a seat in the waiting area. *The singsong of her charming Welsh accent will make my daughter feel at ease,* I thought, as I wiped the sweat off my hands. I felt relieved that Tom had reacted calmly when Fiona had told him about her bulimia the night before.

At first, the nurse spoke with Fiona in private. Fifteen minutes later, Tom and I were invited to join them on sanitary plastic chairs set up in a circle. A second nurse entered the room.

"Call me Theresa," she shrilled.

With her ridiculously purple hair, bright red glasses, and stern look, she reminded me of one of those wannabe liberal types, who thought the colour of her hair could build connections with teenagers. I wasn't impressed.

"Fiona, hi, thank you for coming to see us. You're so brave," Theresa said. "Let's get you weighed."

Fiona barely glanced up from her fidgeting hands. Despite the summer weather, she was dressed in her dark-blue school uniform sweatshirt. It needed a wash, but she was determined to wear it. Maybe she felt less vulnerable in this huge thing.

Emily grabbed her clipboard and got up. She asked Fiona to hop on the

CHAPTER 1

scale in the far corner of the room. Anxiously I drew my eyebrows together. In theory, nobody in our family should know their exact weight, because I'd never seen the point in wasting money on buying scales. We estimated our weight according to our clothes sizes. So, when Dr. Stevens had told Fiona that she weighed 63 kg recently, she had reacted with tears. It was highly unlikely that her weight would have gone up in the meantime, but you never knew, scales were not always accurate.

Fortunately, Emily was smart enough to cover the numbers on the sliders with her hand and not to say Fiona's weight aloud. Off to a good start.

Everybody sat upright, except my husband. He leaned back in his chair and a little to one side as if this were a corporate boardroom meeting. Suntanned and in a white dress shirt, he looked his absolute best.

Theresa, turning to him while she spoke, ran over the bulimic binge-purge cycle. Food restriction leads to cravings; they in turn lead to binge eating and feelings of guilt, which trigger purging, she explained.

"In order to break the cycle, Fiona needs to eat regularly," she said. "Every three hours. She needs to have breakfast, lunch, dinner, and two snacks in between meals. Don't allow her to use the toilet for about twenty to thirty minutes after she's eaten. Then you can relax, because once that time has gone by, it'll be almost impossible for Fiona to throw up her food. Do you understand?"

"Absolutely," my husband said.

Emily turned to Fiona.

"Your blood results have come back as normal, and your weight is normal, too. There's nothing we should be worried about. Your loving parents will support you with your eating. You'll be fine. We'll see you back here after Christmas."

After Christmas? It's only November. Surely, she must be kidding. I frowned.

"Bearing in mind the upcoming holidays," Emily said, "Fiona won't be seeing our psychiatrist until the middle of January. Therapy will begin after that. Do you have any questions?"

"Er ... no ..." Tom said. "Everything is under control."

For crying out loud! Why did he say that? Does he really believe everything is fine or is he too ashamed to admit that we have no clue how to help our struggling daughter? It was hard to tell with him. My head spun.

The only reason why Fiona had stopped making herself sick was because I was watching her like a hawk. But what if she wanted to leave the house to spend time with her friends? Or at Anthony's? How was this all supposed to work? Nobody had asked if *I* perhaps needed to go to work. I could just tell those nurses weren't interested in how we managed, especially after Tom's reaction. And why hadn't we discussed any of the *causes* of Fiona's bulimia?

Do Emily and Theresa really believe that making Fiona eat lots of food is all we need to do to magically fix her eating disorder?

"I'd like her to see a *psychologist* instead of a psychiatrist," I said.

"An appointment with a psychologist? That's a six-month wait," snapped Theresa, her red glasses slipping to the tip of her nose.

"That can't be right," I replied, shocked, but the nurses nodded.

How many people commit suicide because of these long waiting times?

"Is there anything else we can do to help Fiona?" I tried to sound polite.

Emily and Theresa shook their heads, stood up, and shook our hands.

"Have a good Christmas," they said, and patted Fiona on the shoulder.

She had done so well, Theresa said.

Aw, yes, fuck off.

If there was one thing I hated, it was those belittling comments. I was also angry with myself. I should have pushed both women against the wall and demanded to see a specialist before the holidays. But I didn't want to cause a scandal in front of Fiona. She needed to feel assured, thinking that we truly had everything under control, and Tom, by sounding so confident, had achieved that. After the appointment, he drove to Christchurch without saying anything further about the session, trusting that I would stay on top of things.

All of last week, I'd been painting the outside of our house. It was a time-consuming job, and I'd planned on finishing it after seeing the mental health nurses. Therefore, it was already eight o'clock when I carried pots with steaming rice and chicken curry to the dinner table. We didn't always eat that late, but we certainly always ate together. Dinner was treated like a social

CHAPTER 1

event. It meant gathering around the table, talking about the day, discussing world issues, and gossiping.

Tonight, Eric was the first one at the table. He served himself a massive portion. I asked him to wait for everyone. A minute later, Fiona and Anthony emerged from her bedroom.

"Sorry, Tony," I said. "It's rice tonight."

"I'll eat the curry with the leftover pasta then," he said, standing in front of the fridge with both doors wide open until it started beeping.

"Tony, be quick," I said. "You're wasting electricity. Take whatever you want. The pasta is on the bottom shelf behind the bread, I think."

Fiona pushed her body in front of his. With a cheerful teenage screech in her voice, she proclaimed that she was over eating rice, too. She snatched a yoghurt off the shelf and sat down. She'd eaten well today, and she hadn't purged, so I let the yoghurt pass for dinner.

While we ate, I noticed with relief that her mood had picked up. Tom and the mental health nurses were right; there was no reason to stress. I was overthinking things. The kids would always mock me for that. I did it with everything.

Then, after dinnertime, I took my laptop to bed, typed *bulimia facts* in the search bar, and started reading. It was difficult to get reliable numbers on bulimia because there was no official authority that kept track of bulimia cases, and many people with bulimia never sought professional help. Nevertheless, millions of people around the world were affected by this mental illness. Only about half of them ever recover.

Half? That can't be right.

My stomach tightened. I went on a different website to verify. There it said only thirty-five percent fully recover.

There is no way in hell that my precious girl will live with this illness for the rest of her life. I must make sure of that!

My eyes further skimmed the page. Eating disorders have the highest mortality rate of any psychiatric illnesses. *What!? Wow!* If Fiona wasn't able to keep her food down, potassium levels could plummet, triggering her heart to stop. Her oesophagus could rupture. This could also be fatal.

I slammed the laptop shut with such force that I thought for an instant I had broken it. Why did we have to wait until mid-January? Tom and the nurses were definitely taking it too lightly. *Fiona's life is in our hands!* I slid under the covers, clasped my husband's pillow and pressed it against my stomach. *I won't leave her out of my sight, not for a split second, not until we have proper help,* I promised myself, although I knew full well that this was a fairy-tale idea.

Chapter 2

Today would be the school's prize-giving ceremony. The morning was nerve-wracking because Fiona refused to leave the house. It took me hours to convince her.

"Even if you go merely out of respect for the other students," I'd said.

At the last minute she gave in, pulled her heavy uniform sweatshirt over her head and climbed in the car with me. The humidity in my silver Volkswagen was unbearable.

"Mum, roll the windows down!" she yelled.

"Why the hell are you wearing that stupid sweatshirt then?" I shouted back at her.

"Cos."

"Ridiculous." I shook my head.

We didn't speak to each other for the rest of the ride. When we arrived at school, she perked up and rushed to take a seat next to her friends. Anthony sat behind her. He was called to come up on stage several times that morning, being awarded one sports trophy after the other. Each time, Fiona turned her head to throw me one of those proud looks.

Dr. Stevens sat in the row in front of me. I recognised him straight away. His boy was in the year group above my daughter's. *How convenient having a doctor present*, I thought, because I felt a little faint. There was no air-conditioning or ventilation in the assembly hall despite a whopping thirty-three degrees outside. The hall was packed with students and their parents, whose transpiration added to the swelter.

I, too, was sweating, not so much because of the heat, as I was wearing a light summer dress, but because of the morning's stress.

About an hour into the ceremony, the chairman of the board of trustees stood up to announce the Year 11 top scholars.

"Could Emily Albert, Max Camden, and Fiona Elison please come forward," he said.

The instant my daughter's name was mentioned, my heels lifted off the ground, and my heart skipped a beat, but at the same time my chest tightened.

Did you hear that, doctor? shot through my head. *My daughter is a top scholar. She's brighter than your son.* I have always known she's a smart girl. In fact, she's one of those all-rounders: academic, athletic, and kind. A parents' delight. And just in case you were wondering: This bulimia thing? It came out of the blue. Like a virus. It caught her by surprise.

Dr. Stevens was looking fixedly at the front, unaware that I sat behind him, let alone talked to him in my imagination. Both of us saw how Fiona crossed the stage from left to right with her eyes lowered, her feet barely touching the ground, and her hand barely touching the congratulating hand of the principal. I didn't see her smile, and when I heard the applause, my eyes started to burn. Dr. Stevens clapped, but my own hands clung tightly to the prize-giving program.

On the way home, I told Fiona how proud I was of her, but she didn't say much. She was fretting about the upcoming external exams. I offered her my support, and I was glad that she accepted my help. Together we worked out a study plan, I printed a stack of practice exams, and we made flashcards for vocabulary and formulas for maths. We broke the study load down into small chunks and her study time into twenty-minute intervals. But every time I checked on her, I would find her resting on her bed, mindlessly scrolling through her feeds. She voiced that she wasn't going to sit her exams this year, because she already had enough credits to pass. I was confused. I clearly remembered a time when she had tooted to the whole family that she was looking forward to exams.

"Why don't you go to at least one of them?" I asked.

"I can't focus," she responded. "Please, Mum, I don't want to go."

"But you're such a clever girl."

CHAPTER 2

"It's too hard," she said and burst into tears.

It must be the sadness about her illness that is making her mind go off track, I thought. Although she was eating regularly now, not huge amounts but enough, and although I wouldn't let her use the bathroom after the meals, it did nothing to change her irritability and her wish to lose weight.

In the absence of therapy, I decided to talk with her about body image. I was convinced that once she understood how beautiful she was, she would be able to relax, eat, and study.

"I really don't like my legs," Fiona said the moment I brought up the subject.

"But your legs are fine. All right, they're not twigs, they're muscular because you've danced for so many years, and you've played volleyball, and you ran. Look, you've got the beautiful legs of an athlete."

"No, they're fat."

"They're not. They're skinny. Much skinnier than your girlfriends' legs, can't you see that?"

"Not really."

I sighed softly. This bulimia thing was making her blind. There was no point in arguing with her.

"Look, Poppy, there will always be something we don't like about ourselves. But we have to learn to live with it. When I was your age, I had huge gaps between my teeth. I looked like Bugs Bunny when I smiled."

"I know. But you got them fixed, didn't you?"

"When I was eighteen, Fiona."

"Whatever."

I could feel this conversation going in the wrong direction, therefore I suggested that we should watch the short video clip that I had found the night before.

"Could we watch it on your phone?"

"Okay."

Fiona was lying on her bed. I plopped next to her.

"Why don't you google Natalie Patterson? She recites this poem called 'I have a beautiful body.' She is Afro-American and ..."

"Found it."

Fiona held up her phone so we could both see the poet while listening to her voice.

"*... you have a beautiful body, have implies ownership meaning I ... own something I never paid for ... meaning I didn't earn it - so I don't know the value of ...*"

Click.

"Not interested, Mother!" She threw her phone on the ground and rolled onto her side turning her back to me.

For the first time since her diagnosis, this odd feeling, that she had become someone else because I had intruded her space, came over me. Discreetly I got up from the bed, and for a brief moment stood motionless next to it. *Perhaps if I disappear quietly, my girl could safely re-inhabit her body*, ran through my head. Then I noticed despair uncoiling in my stomach, or was it grief? It was tempting to say something consoling to her, but I said nothing, and then I tiptoed out of the room and closed the door softly behind me.

It was after midnight on the same day. I was awake, ruminating about the past year, checking whether I could have caught this bulimia thing when it still had been feeble and much easier to destroy.

The previous summer had been overshadowed by the sudden passing of my brother. Eric and Fiona had enjoyed a close relationship with their Uncle Oliver. They had felt honoured that he would endure dreadful long-haul flights from Europe just to be with them. They knew that he found New Zealand boring, being the big city intellectual that he was. Nevertheless, he would turn up every year, his suitcase filled with sweets, new card games, and other exciting trinkets. During his stay, he'd entertain the children with soccer matches in the backyard, maths quizzes, and his overall quirky personality. They both adored him, Fiona perhaps even more so than Eric. Even as a twelve-year-old, she was impressed by her uncle's achievements. He'd written a doctoral thesis in mathematics about dimensions and spaces ordinary humans were unable to conceptualise. So she would walk around calling her uncle a genius, and she would make herself look important when she pronounced the word "genius." Shortly before he died, Fiona had made plans to spend an exchange year in Munich. He would take her under his wing, he had promised, and invite her to sports events and concerts. But then the plan evaporated.

"Why do you tell people about Uncle Oliver's death?' Fiona had asked back in December. The usual kindness in her voice was gone. "It's none of their business."

"Well, it's the way I deal with things. I talk," I said.

"You're embarrassing."

"Better than bottling things up."

I had a reason for saying that. After all, wasn't that what my brother had been doing, covering up his problems before he took his life? But Fiona didn't know that, of course. She thought that he had died from a heart attack.

I had encouraged Fiona to speak to one of the councillors at school about her grief. She went once, but she didn't see Jane Paladino.

"I don't want to talk about my emotions. I hate it," she'd said and pulled a face.

So little by little, we tried to come to grips with the grief, each on our own, or sometimes together, hoping that time would heal the emotional wounds.

Barely two months after the funeral, Fiona's boyfriend, Marc, rejected her. The one person who had distracted her from the grief with his teenage silliness was now gone, too. It gnawed on her self-esteem.

Fortunately, as the weeks went by, Anthony, the most popular senior boy in Fiona's high school, replaced Marc, and the dull car rides home from school reverted back into the lively ones that they had always been.

Once we got to the house, Anthony would bang on Eric's apartment door. If Eric wasn't on night shift, he would pretend that he was annoyed with Anthony for interrupting the superhero movie that he had already watched a million times. They would exchange a few words, then Fiona and Anthony would hurry to hide in her bedroom or sit wrapped up in blankets in our so-called Netflix room, a separate lounge with an enormous TV, watching something. And I would be the one in charge of the dinner that needed cooking. We would all come together to eat at about six o'clock.

Then Eric, Fiona, and Anthony would disperse again to the same places as before. I would stack the dishwasher, clean the kitchen table and counter tops, and climb upstairs to the spacious landing area in front of the master bedroom. I would kick back in a bean bag, reading or texting Tom. Around nine o'clock, the four of us would congregate again in the open-plan kitchen.

By that time Fiona would already have prepared a second feed for Anthony. Typically, one of those ready-to-bake pizza bases with tomato sauce, chopped vegetables, and grated cheese on top. Eric had the habit of pinching one or two slices and brewing himself a black tea, while Fiona and I would sit close together at the wooden kitchen table, sipping on green tea and observing Anthony devour his late-night meal. Neither of us would see the flicker of envy in Fiona's starving eyes. And neither of us would hear the hungry screams inside her head that must have been making it hard for her to understand Eric's jokes, the silly ones that he had heard at work.

Sometimes we would need to coordinate our weekly schedules because neither Fiona nor Anthony had their driver's license yet, and we lived rural. On one of those evenings, I asked Fiona when she wanted me to pick her and Anthony up from the party that night.

"It's not a party," she said rolling her eyes and grinning at Anthony. "It's *drinks*. How many times do I have to tell you this?"

"All right, *drinks*."

"At two, if that's okay with you."

"No problem," I said. "By the way, how's Dan?"

"Fine."

"Why are ya asking about Dan?" Anthony glanced back and forth at Fiona and me.

"Oh, last Saturday when Mum picked me up, we also took Dan, Matt, and Dylan home. Dan was so wasted, Mum told him that he'd have to clean her car if he threw up. It was so funny. He called her Mama Fiona all the way home, because he had forgotten her name. And whenever we'd turn around a corner, he'd sway from side to side and scream, 'Mama Fiona, don't drive so fast!' We were in stitches."

"Good old Danny boy," Anthony said. "He's always a laugh. By the way, I think you should sign up with Uber, Selina."

"No thanks. Picking up you guys every weekend is trouble enough."

CHAPTER 2

"Come on, Mum, stop pretending you don't enjoy it. I know you love picking up drunk teenagers."

We all laughed. Fiona was right. I enjoyed young people, sober or not, because they still had flexible minds filled with innocent ideas about their future. I also enjoyed that no matter how late we came home, Fiona would always have a hot drink before going to bed and tattle about the little party dramas. She knew I would find her stories amusing. When Anthony stayed over after the party, he would talk over Fiona. She would have to tell him a thousand times to shut up. He never did when he was drunk. Long into the night, I would hear him babble to himself while Fiona would be right beside him fast asleep, and I would laugh to myself.

And so, the months had passed with one week not being much different from another. The images that I had stored in my mind of these weekday afternoons and evenings knitted together into a picture of a harmonious life. Fiona and I had never argued much. And whenever I had heard other parents talk about their rude teenage daughters who shut themselves off from them, I had felt blessed because it seemed such a horrible thing to have to go through.

However, five months pre-diagnosis, the painful vision of hindsight revealed to me that, one evening in June, I could have put an end to Fiona's lonely suffering. She had called me into her bedroom. One quick glance at her was enough to tell me that she'd been crying. I could see that her cheeks were red and soft, almost puffy, even though the room was gloomy with her small desk light barely shining on her face. She appeared small, as if she had shrunk, and forlorn, the way she was kneeling in the middle of her queen-size bed. She said she wanted to see a councillor.

"But what's wrong?" I was taken by surprise. "Did something bad happen?"

She couldn't say. "I'm just sad, Mummy."

"What about?"

"Everything. Life."

"Well, I guess we all feel a kind of sentimental sadness sometimes. I think, as a little kid, you're oblivious to the problems that challenge the world, but as a teenager, your vision changes. You suddenly realise that society isn't perfect and that there's much suffering in the world. That's the painful part of becoming an adult, I guess. In German, we have a wonderful word for this feeling. It's called *Weltschmerz*. Everybody feels that sometimes. I do, too."

And Fiona had nodded her head and then dried her tears.

Now I believe that deep inside, though, she had hoped that I would guess the real reason for her agony, expose the binge eating and purging, and rescue her from the claws of this debilitating illness because she herself wasn't able to talk about it. Her desire to please me and the shame that had come with her illness had sealed her mouth shut.

And I had been blinded by our trusting relationship. I hadn't dug deeper. I hadn't seen the pleading in her red eyes, the same eyes that now, months later, were looking at me again and torturing me.

It's dangerous to stir up these memories, because I can't go back and change things. I must get some sleep now.

Christmas was coming up fast. Knowing that nobody in the family was in the mood for "Jingle Bells", and that Fiona would feel uncomfortable around copious amounts of cakes and meats, I contemplated taking the family on a trip abroad.

We should spend the week before the festive season on a beach somewhere instead of getting presents, then skip Christmas at home, I suggested to Tom over the phone. He agreed and said he would prefer an island trip to a traditional Christmas anytime. It hardly took me an hour to find a cheap vacation deal, call Anthony's mother to ask for permission to take her son along, and book the trip. Pleased with myself for having bought flight tickets in lieu of a glazed ham and pavlova, I was slouching on one of the sofas when Fiona and Anthony came running upstairs.

"Whatcha doin', Selina?" Anthony asked.

"Guess what, guys? We are flying to V-a-n-u-aaaa-t-u."

"No way! Oh, my God!" Fiona leaped on the sofa and squeezed me. "When are we going?"

"We'll be there in two weeks."

"Just the other day, Tony and I were looking at Vanuatu in your travel atlas!"

CHAPTER 2

"I know. I was in the living room folding laundry, when you were on the sofa ripping the book out of each other's hands."

"Is Tony coming, too?"

"Of course he is. We're all going. The whole family, " I said.

"Whoopee!" Fiona gave me a flighty kiss on the head, then she jumped up and embraced Anthony with one of those bear hugs. He stood like a mummy stuck to the ground and stared at me in disbelief. It was comical to see him speechless.

"For how long are we going?" Fiona asked.

"Six days."

"Oh, my God! You're the best!" she squealed.

"I've called your mum," I said to Anthony. "She's fine with it. And don't worry about money, my boy. I still owe you for taking Fiona to the councillor. You're invited."

"For real?" he sounded incredulous.

"Yep."

"Thank you." He finally smiled.

Fiona grabbed his arms and pulled him down the stairs. "Party time!" she yelled, and then she cranked up their hideous drum and bass music to celebrate.

Even before we arrived on the main island, Vanuatu gave us something to talk about during those tricky mealtimes. Anthony, who'd never been abroad, asked a million times about what to pack, and he researched top things to do. Fiona announced one night that she wanted to go to the rock pools on the first day. Anthony spoke over her, saying that he'd like to go on a zipline ride, maybe on the same day or the next. Content, I listened to their chatter.

As soon as we arrived, we were hit by a humid heat that unstuck my anxious and stiff body. Suddenly I realised that I hadn't properly relaxed since I'd received the news from Jane Paladino, almost eight weeks ago.

Here on the island, there was no need for me to freak out when Fiona was out of sight. I knew she would either be with Eric, Tom, or Anthony or any combination of them. I was also able to withdraw from my cooking responsibilities. Breakfast and lunch were prepared by the hotel staff. In the evenings, we ate out. Fiona would choose the same meal options every day - tropical fruit, pasta, and salads - but that didn't worry me. She ate.

Halfway through the trip, we decided one afternoon to chill by the hotel pool. Tom and I unwound on the sun loungers while Eric, Fiona, and Anthony chased each other around the pool, totally ignoring the "Walk, Don't Run" rule.

"Sun's up, float is out!" I heard Anthony yell.

Happily, I watched the three for a while as they dove in and out of the water like human seals. Then I closed my eyes. The warm sun felt soothing on my naked skin. The smell of suntan oil added to the holiday feel. I thought about earlier that day when we were in town buying mangoes at the market. I had taken pleasure in observing the locals who sat behind their stalls. Some of them were scrolling their phones, and I was curious as to what their Instagram feeds showed.

Would they also be looking at super skinny, white-legged girl models? Or did they find them repulsive? The perception of beauty varies from culture to culture. It was hard to imagine teenagers on Vanuatu obsessing about wanting to be skinny. I bet they had probably never heard of such a thing as bulimia. Could this mean that an eating disorder was a man-made illness, something that only grew in privileged minds? To starve yourself or to chuck up food on purpose must seem such an insane idea to someone who finds being skinny undesirable or to someone for whom poverty-related malnutrition is a reality.

We should move to Vanuatu until Fiona is better, I thought, when all of a sudden, I felt water dripping onto my stomach. I opened my eyes and saw Fiona leaning over me. She was wringing her hair out.

"Please, no! I don't want to get wet right now."

She laughed.

"Do you want to go to the beach tonight to watch the fire show and have cocktails?" I asked her.

"Sure," she said and sat down on the edge of the sun lounger.

"After that, we'll drink kava with the locals," Tom said.

"Not me. I'm not drinking kava," Anthony shouted.

"You've never tried," Fiona shouted back.

CHAPTER 2

"Yeah, we'll make him," Eric said.

Later at the hotel, the young ones fell asleep with their clothes still on, whipped from all the action. After the fire show, Tom had played pool with them. Anthony had tried the kava and spat it back out. Fiona had smiled for the camera. She hadn't done this in months. What a great night out it had been! I turned on my stomach and searched for Tom's hand under the sheets. Fiona was so safe here.

We recently had returned from Vanuatu, and I was grocery shopping at our local supermarket because the pantry needed stocking up.

It was only ten o'clock in the morning.

Suddenly, this text appeared: *Mum, I'm in an ambulance. Can you pick me up from the hospital?*

What happened? R u OK? I texted back.

Fainted at work. I'm good. Love you.

Holy heck, I thought, *why is she in an ambulance?* I quit shopping and raced to the hospital, a twenty-minute drive from town. The instant I arrived, the physician on call took me to one side. He touched my elbow when he told me quietly that the warehouse employees who had seen Fiona collapse were certain that she had had a seizure. Her legs had jerked uncontrollably. She'd peed herself. I believed those people, because in one of my books about bulimia, I had read that not all patients who purge have abnormal lab results, meaning if she still purged occasionally, she was at high risk of dehydration, which potentially causes seizures. Normal lab results meant nothing.

And so, apparently, Fiona wasn't as fine as the mental health nurses had thought she was, but I didn't say anything to her. She was terrified enough as it was. She claimed she had fainted from the scorching heat in the warehouse. She also said she didn't want to return to the summer job she had just started because she was too ashamed after today's incident. I understood.

Not much longer and we would see the psychiatrist.

I am glad I don't remember his name. He was one of those weak-looking men, who as a child was always picked last for team sports. His pants were too short, displaying socks which so obviously didn't match that I wondered if they were a political statement. For the first thirty minutes, he talked with Fiona behind closed doors. When he reappeared, he said he had about five minutes left to spend with me, two minutes of which he wasted confirming my details and asking me about Fiona's birth.

"It was a peaceful water birth in a spa surrounded by candlelight." I wasn't lying.

"And her childhood, what was that like?"

"Gosh, better than mine," I scoffed. "She spent a lot of time playing outside. We used to live on a large property with a small paddock and a forested area .... what's it called again? .... erm, a lifestyle block, with lambs, ducks, chooks, you name it. She always had friends. We also travelled a lot. She has seen the world."

He scribbled something on the notepad that rested on his knees.

"I think puberty was difficult for her," I continued. "We moved houses a few times, and she had to say goodbye to the friends she'd made. Then her uncle died ..."

"Sorry to interrupt, Mrs. Elison, but I must shoot to my next appointment. After talking to your daughter, I get the impression that she's suffering from depression. I'll give you a prescription for antidepressants. She said she'd stopped binge eating and purging. I'd say she's historically bulimic. Next week, she'll start cognitive behavioural therapy with Emily and Theresa. In the meantime, make sure she continues to eat regularly. I'll see her again in six months."

He stood up and waited for a short moment. Delighted that I wasn't saying anything, he smiled, gave me the prescription, and shook my hand.

"Nice meeting you and your lovely daughter," he said and exited the room.

My body tensed. I was speechless. I felt like picking up a chair and throwing it against the wall. But this wasn't a movie, and Fiona stood waiting for me outside the room.

"How was the chat with the psychiatrist?" I asked her casually while we walked to my car.

"All right," she said. "He asked about my childhood and stuff."

"Good that therapy will start shortly."

"Mm-hmm."

"Do you want to be dropped off at Anthony's for a few hours?"

I needed to be on my own.

"Yes, please."

I could swear I broke every speed limit on the way from Anthony's place to our home, tears streaming down my face. As soon as I got through the door, I poured myself a glass of pinot gris, took a huge gulp, and patrolled around the massive park-like garden that surrounded our two-story house with the wine in my hand, yelling in my head at the psychiatrist.

"Historically bulimic." What kind of a lame expression is that? Historically ... really? Oh, why don't you live in my house for a week, you stupid Dr. blah, blah, blah.... I'll show you historically! The poor girl has no life anymore. You can see it in her face. She's constantly preoccupied with food, calories, her legs, whatever, probably thinking about how to hide her binge eating and purging. I don't care what your textbooks say. People don't just stop something they've been doing for ten months, I mean, every day for ten months, and ta-da, they're cured.

"Ridiculous!" I screamed out loud.

I called Tom. "The man is an idiot."

"Look, honey, I understand that you're mad, but let Fiona start with therapy."

"Yes, but there's no way I'm giving her antidepressants. She's not depressed!"

"Well, then don't. When is the first session?"

"Wednesday. After that, school starts, and I'll be working. Anthony might have to keep an eye on her during lunchtimes. Jesus, what would we do without that boy?"

"She'll get better with therapy."

"I hope so, Tom."

Unfortunately, Fiona's mental well-being spiralled down quite rapidly. During the first week back at school, I saw her face peek through the small window of my classroom door while I was relief teaching a geography lesson. It was the last lesson of the day; nevertheless, we still had twenty minutes to go. I tried to ignore her. A few minutes passed. Her face had disappeared, but my phone vibrated.

Mum, I need to go home.

I broke out in a sweat. The thirty fourteen-year-olds I was supervising were a wound-up bunch, capable of killing each other the moment I turned my back on them. While keeping an eye on the class, I rushed to the door and opened it. I saw Fiona sitting on the concrete, shaking. It looked as if she were having a breakdown.

"Come on, darling, get up and sit at my desk," I said in a calm voice.

With the back of her hands, she quickly wiped a tear off her face, then she dragged herself into the classroom. She sat down at one of the desks in the front corner near me. Fortunately, the students knew that she was my daughter and none of them said anything.

Initially, I thought this was going to be a one-off incident, but it repeated itself every couple of days or so. If she wasn't crying, she would be cold and shaky, or feel dizzy. Sometimes she complained about chest pains. I asked Fiona to address her breakdowns in her next therapy session. She later reported to me that when she did, Theresa reacted in the most appalling way.

"She told me to get over my teenage shit!" Fiona shouted. "I'm *never* going back to her."

I swallowed hard. It was time to explore alternative options. We had waited far too long, given that the chance of recovering from an eating disorder decreases the later it is treated. When I spoke to Tom, he suggested that we should look abroad for help.

"Yes, I think they have special clinics for eating-disorder patients in the US. I remember seeing something like that on TV," I said.

"We could send her over for a month."

"Do you think one month is long enough? I'd have to accompany her."

"We'll do whatever it takes, honey."

"It would be hugely expensive. Not sure if we can afford it. We would have to get a small loan maybe. Let me check first if I can find a private psychologist before we look for help elsewhere. Or maybe we send her to Aussie? Don't they have clinics?"

"All right, honey, you call around. I've gotta run now. Talk to you tomorrow. When are you leaving for your retreat? Saturday?"

"Yes, Saturday morning."

"Right. After your retreat, I'll have two more weeks left in Christchurch, and then I'll wrap it up. Paul said they can shift me to a project closer to home. I told you that, didn't I?"

"Yes, you did. And I am glad."

After the phone call, I devoted the rest of the day to Fiona. She had curled up on her bed like a scared kitten. I settled next to her with my laptop on my legs. An online bulimia self-help manual caught my attention. I downloaded it and studied the first module while stroking her back.

"We'll get this figured out, Poppy."

She didn't react, but that was okay. Suddenly the idea of a therapy dog popped into my head. A dog would love her unconditionally, regardless of her body shape, weight, leg size, mood, and whatever else.

"Would you like to get a puppy?"

Excitedly she lifted her head.

"Why don't you check online if you can find labradoodle puppies for sale?"

"I want a brown one," she said and stretched her arm out to reach for her phone.

During the days that followed, I called psychologists and eating disorder specialists until I couldn't bear it anymore.

"I'm sorry, Mrs. Elison, but we have a waiting list. Do you want me to put your daughter's name on it?"

"Yes, please."

"She has bulimia, you said?"

"Yes."

"The wait can be very long. We give priority to patients with anorexia."

Every phone call ended like this.

Chapter 3

On a promising day, Fiona would go to school and I would be alone in the house. I would make a coffee, stand at the large kitchen windows, and stare into the wattle trees on the neighbouring property. I could never recall for how long I stood there, paranoid that I might find Fiona dead in her bed one day because her stomach had ruptured, or her heart had stopped beating. Fear had altered my perception of time.

It was the beginning of March 2020. COVID-19 had arrived in New Zealand, and the country shut its borders to the outside world. We were trapped inside. It would have been extremely complicated to travel overseas for professional help.

Desperately, I continued to study the bulimia self-help manual for home therapy ideas. I had overheard people say that one never fully recovers from bulimia. Although I knew this wasn't true, I worried that it could become true the longer we waited.

Over the weekend, Tom and I agreed that for a while we could survive on his salary only. Come Monday morning, I called the assistant principal of Fiona's high school and explained that I would no longer be able to relief teach. I was needed at home, I said.

Later that day, I had an appointment with Fiona's dean, Diane. She was a tall woman with an intense voice and a loud genuine laugh. Her charismatic presence filled the staff room in no time. She enjoyed the reputation of going above and beyond for her students, yet she could be too much for some of her colleagues. But I admired her strength and felt comfortable about meeting her.

CHAPTER 3

When I walked into Diane's office, she was buzzing around with a stack of photocopies in one hand and her cell phone in the other. Her face brightened as she greeted me. She freed her hands to point me to an old chair next to her desk and took a seat herself. Then she turned towards me and leaned forward. I knew I had her full attention. I began to explain the real reason for Fiona's frequent absences since the beginning of term.

"Sometimes the disturbing thoughts about her appearance overwhelm her. It's like she has a voice inside her head that, when it grows too loud, forces her to leave the classroom. Anyway, that's how she explained it to me. It must be similar to experiencing high levels of anxiety. She usually texts me when that happens, and I jump in my car and get her straight away," I said.

While I spoke, I noticed a pained look appearing on Diane's face. She declared that she had no knowledge about eating disorders, but she took her time asking sensible questions.

I queried if we could come to a special arrangement about Fiona's absences.

"As long as she signs herself out and we know where she is, it's fine," Diane said. "Fiona is such a gifted student. She'll catch up."

"I really appreciate this," I said. "Often, she leaves before lunch because she doesn't feel comfortable eating in front of her friends. She thinks that they keep track of what she eats and judge her. The poor girl compares all the time. She compares the size of their lunches to hers. She is hyper aware of how much everybody eats. It's mad."

"Poor darling."

"A few of the girls she hangs out with starve themselves throughout the school day. It's such a thing these days, and then they stuff themselves at a fast food restaurant once school has finished."

"Do you think it would help if she came to my office for lunch?" she asked curiously.

"Hmm. I'm not sure," I said. "I can ask her. None of her friends know about her eating disorder yet, so I'm afraid they might wonder why she's eating in your office." I paused. "Another thing is that in the afternoons she loses focus. Her body is exhausted by then. And on some days, she doesn't even make it to school in the first place."

"I'm so sorry to hear that." She drew her eyebrows together. "Honestly, if she needs to stay home or go home early, I'll explain her. And if there's anything else I can do, please let me know." She shook her head. "Poor petal."

We both stood up. Diane opened her mouth to say something else, but then she paused and smiled at me instead. Her hand touched my shoulder. I looked at the butterfly tattoo on her neck to avoid meeting her eyes.

"How are you coping with all of this?" she finally asked.

For an instant, I was tempted to pour my heart out to her. *She would understand,* I said to myself. *It would do me good to talk to her.* I quickly glanced at the clock on her wall. Any minute now the bell would ring, and she would have to dash off to teach her next lesson. I pressed my lips together, clenched my car keys and phone, raised my eyes to look at her and said, "I'm doing fine, Diane, really. And thank you for being so supportive."

That night after dinner, I knocked on Fiona's bedroom door to ask her if she needed a snack and if she wanted me to keep her company. I had been doing this for several weeks now. Whenever she was at home, I would check on her roughly every two hours because I didn't want her to be sitting alone in her quiet bedroom with her loud thoughts—and because I was permanently nervous.

Fiona shook her head. She wasn't hungry, she said.

I sat down on her bed and cautiously suggested that we work a bit on her eating disorder. She agreed, perhaps because she was bored with looking at her social media feed. It was hard to tell.

"Let's find a piece of paper and write down what sort of things you value the most in your life," I started.

"I don't want to write anything down."

"All right, we can just talk about it then. Tell me what matters most to you."

"Not sure," she answered. But after a few minutes of silence, she said: "My family."

"Good. What else?"

"Having fun and being with my friends."

"Family, friends, and what else?"

CHAPTER 3

"School, because I want to go to uni."

"You've always really enjoyed school, haven't you?" I smiled.

Fiona didn't react.

"You know, Poppy," I looked at her fondly, "Mum, Dad and your brother, Eric, love you because of who you are. We aren't worried about your weight. You're a beautiful girl, inside and out. And your friends like you because of your personality, your humour, your kindness, all those things."

"Mm-hmm." She shrugged her shoulders.

"Do you think you'd lose your friends if you gained weight? Say Eva would gain three kilos. Besides the fact that you probably wouldn't even notice, you'd still have her as your best friend, wouldn't you?"

Fiona pulled up her legs. She hugged her knees, rested her head on them and looked at me sideways. Her lips quivered.

"The bulimia voice demands so much from you. Can you see that?" I said quietly. "I mean, we all like to look good, I get it, but not at such a high cost. You shouldn't have to sacrifice the things that you value for your looks. At the moment, the bulimia voice asks you to destroy your health, to miss school, and it sucks the joy out of your relationships with family and friends. You're not happy anymore, Fiona."

She nodded her head. Tears swelled up in her eyes. She understood.

For a few seconds, I placed my hand on one of her arms and suggested that she keep a food diary. This was regarded as an essential element of most therapies for eating disorders. It would allow her to track hunger, levels of fullness, mood, and thoughts so she could identify what precisely triggered behaviours such as stress eating or urges to binge. And it could assist her with making a change, I pointed out. She nodded again. Personally, I hoped a diary also would allow me to gain fresh insights into her reasoning, which still made such little sense to me.

During the days that followed our conversation, I saw Fiona sitting at her desk a few times. She drew geometrical patterns on pieces of paper, but she never wrote a single word. I didn't push her. Secretly, I sympathised with her. I understood why she didn't want to write about something she was obsessed with and yet wanted to run away from at the same time.

Determined to find an alternative way to slip into her mind, I read a book written by a young American woman who'd suffered from bulimia for eight years. She swore that conventional therapies for eating disorders didn't help her heal, but a program that compared binge eating to drug addiction and treated it as such did help. It assumed that the driving force behind any addiction, and in the young woman's case her compulsive binging, was the reward system of the primitive part of the brain. It drove her binge eating by making her falsely believe that huge amounts of sugary and fatty foods were essential for her survival. The program asked her not to give in to these bodily impulses, and she was able to refrain from doing so because she learnt to distinguish between the voice of the primitive part of the brain that ordered her to binge eat, and the rational part of her brain. The rational voice was asked to argue with the primitive voice and to refuse the execution of the order to binge. So, she didn't get up to open the fridge door and grab huge amounts of food. Instead she sat out the urges, which she knew would pass. Over time, this method allowed her to recover.

I could relate to her story because I knew addiction. From the age of twenty-two to thirty-five, I'd been a heavy smoker. During that time, I was convinced that coffee would never taste the same again without a smoke. Warnings about cancer and leg amputations hadn't deterred me from lighting up one cigarette after another, just like the prospects of osteoporosis, infertility, tooth decay, and other complications weren't stopping Fiona from throwing up her food. Back in the day, those of us who wanted to give up smoking or any addiction wouldn't talk about a rational brain; we called it willpower. But Fiona didn't lack willpower, because if she was able to starve herself for days on end, surely she had more willpower than I ever had.

"Binge eating helps when I feel sad or stressed, like when I don't want to deal with stuff. It kinda numbs me," Fiona said when I discussed the book with her. "And the purging offers relief. It gives me a high."

"A high?"

I was startled. Later I learned that this high after self-induced vomiting is caused by the release of an anti-diuretic hormone called vasopressin which prevents the body from losing too much water and at the same time calms the body. On top of that, Fiona entertained the false belief that by throwing up, she was ridding herself of all the calories that she had consumed during the binge. This would contribute to her feeling alleviated.

"The high doesn't last long," she explained. "Then I feel bad again because I know throwing up is not good for me."

"And it all has become a bit of a habit, would you agree?"

"Maybe. It makes me forget other things."

"But the thoughts that appear to force you to binge, they will eventually pass if you don't act on them. Do you understand that?"

"That's hard, Mum. I've tried." Her voice was brittle, ready to snap any minute. "The problem is that everything in this house reminds me of binge eating."

"I know."

"I hate my bedroom and the kitchen." Then she pleaded to swap rooms with Eric.

Moving downstairs was impractical, of course, because his apartment had a kitchen and a bathroom.

"I hate how our pantry is so close to my bedroom."

I heard anger in her voice now.

"Can we not sell the house?" she asked.

"How about we redecorate your room?"

"That would be sweet," she said, but her smile looked forced, as if a little unsure.

The following morning, we drove into town, selected a delicate Japanese style wallpaper which featured cherry blossom branches and cute little blue birds. It was a perfect new cover for the old walls that had seen too much. We bought soft-coloured, light-blue bedding and pillows that matched, a white desk chair, and a picture frame with white origami butterflies in the shape of a heart, which we hung above her bed. Once finished, we stood with our hands on our hips and looked around the room, satisfied with the outcome.

"Looks nice, I like it," she said and gave me a hug.

"You've got the prettiest room in the house now." I laughed, hopeful that the beautiful environment would positively influence her thoughts.

But the buzz that the refashioned bedroom had brought didn't last long. Only Anthony's company seemed to energise her otherwise lethargic body. Whenever he was around, I heard her voice shriek with joy, I heard laughter, and sometimes arguments. Even so, those were animated, a sign of life. And then, after he left, she was quiet again. Every so often, she would leave her room and sluggishly wander back and forth between the pantry and the fridge, unsure what to eat for a snack. She had stopped designing Instagram-perfect smoothie bowls with chia seeds. She didn't cook or bake anymore. So much about her had changed that I began to suspect that willpower alone was not sufficient to overcome bulimia.

I persisted in raising the eating disorder topic with her, because in my opinion she needed to understand the absurdity of her disturbing thoughts and their subsequent behaviours. Our talks included analysing the causes of her low self-worth and discussing ways of dealing with negative emotions. There were days when Fiona would reason with great ease, and other days when she was immune to reason. That's when she would respond with mumbled indifference or refuse to interact altogether. She would pretend to be tired or yell at me, "Go! Go away!"

And I would quietly withdraw.

Emotionally, my roles as a mother and makeshift therapist became blurred and exhausting. There were times when I thought of myself as a hypocrite because I felt that I was not telling her the truth. What I really wanted to say to her was that she was a stunning looking girl, that her body was perfectly slim with enviably well-proportioned curves, and that the few girls in her year group who were skinnier than her—those with the Kate Moss look—actually looked ill. If only her face wouldn't exhibit such joylessness!

And I wanted to remind her of the thousands of people she had seen walking the streets on her extensive travels. Did they really look like they survived on nothing but cauliflower pizzas and air-fried eggplants? Or was it that stylised, clothes-hanger supermodels clouded what she had seen in person?

And there was something else I really wanted to say to her: I didn't understand how in the hell she was able to make herself spew. It was so revolting.

CHAPTER 3

Roughly two weeks after we had revamped Fiona's bedroom, I was sitting on the balcony reading *The Financial Times* when I caught the smell of the neighbour's barbecue smoke. *Autumn still feels like summer this year*, I thought. My cell phone rang. Instinctively, I jumped up, stepped back inside the house and grabbed the car keys off the sideboard thinking that Fiona needed a pickup. I cast a brief look at the screen. To my surprise, it said "unknown caller ID." I halted in my steps and answered.

"I've got good news for you, Mrs. Elison," said the voice on the other end. "Our eating disorder specialist, Sally Monroe, has accepted your daughter as a patient. Fiona can start sessions next week."

"Whoa! Really? That's fantastic!" I had no idea why I shouted.

"Are you okay with Skype sessions?"

"Of course, yes, I have Skype, yes, no problem. Oh, I'm so happy, so happy!"

"The first session will be three hours long, and we'd like the whole family to be present," she said.

We made arrangements for Wednesday, the 25th of March, because Tom would have moved home from Christchurch by then, and he would still be on vacation.

But when Fiona came home from school, she wasn't pleased.

"I don't want to talk about it in front of Dad," she said. "And Eric. He'll say something stupid."

"He won't, but look, Poppy, Eric doesn't need to be part of the sessions. I'll write to Sally about his speech impairment and that he's on the autism spectrum. You know he'll always support you in his own way, don't you?"

She nodded. "What about Dad?"

"Dad needs to be present. What Sally's practice specialises in is called family-based therapy. They say it's the most successful therapy for adolescents, but it involves Mum *and* Dad."

"I don't think I can do it."

"Yes, you can. Dad won't judge you." I said.

"Still."

"Come, let's go upstairs, I'll show you a photo of Sally. They have one on the practice web page. She looks really friendly."

We both climbed two steps at a time to the upper floor, sat next to each other on the carpet with our backs leaning against the sofa, and I fired up my laptop. Within seconds, Sally's photo popped up, because I had bookmarked the page.

"Oh, yes, she looks nice."

"She has many years of experience," I told her. "She has helped a lot of girls with bulimia. You'll need to trust her. Do you think you can do that?"

"Yes," she said, cracking her knuckles.

I prayed that night that Fiona would be able to connect with the therapist. It was crucial.

Sally was an attractive woman in her late forties with a fringy pixie haircut that complemented the shape of her face. She wore bright pink lipstick and large dangle earrings that looked like dragonfly wings when we had our first therapy session. Fortunately, it was a video call, and we didn't see but could only guess that she had a tall, lean body because sometimes the body shape of the therapist can have an impact on the relationship with an eating-disorder patient.

She greeted us with one of those awkward little Skype waves, her smile radiating warmth. We waved back, sitting strangely squashed together on the lounge sofa.

Tom was putting on a brave face for Fiona. I knew he didn't believe in these sessions. "Counselling bullshit," he'd called it, and I had shrugged my shoulders. Fortunately, he wasn't the one who had to like Sally. I noticed that Fiona was just as nervous as I was. But it didn't take long for Sally to win us over. As soon as she finished introducing herself, our breathing relaxed, and Fiona stopped digging her fingernails into her palms.

Firstly, Sally invited us to speak about what we thought had contributed to Fiona developing the eating disorder. My daughter mentioned that she'd been disliking her body for years. I talked about past events that I thought of as significant. Tom said he didn't know.

After that, we took turns describing how the eating disorder was affecting us. Either pain or embarrassment had reduced Fiona's voice to a whisper.

CHAPTER 3

Sally could barely understand what Fiona was saying. Tom and I confessed how upset we were. Sally didn't comment on anything that we said. She just listened patiently and took notes. It felt nice not being rushed.

She moved on to ask Tom and me about our views on dieting and health food. I told her that I'd never been on a diet, but I also said that we weren't a fast-food family. We ate healthy meals. Tom said something about hoping to lose a few kilos. Sally's facial expressions remained non-judgmental while she unpacked further instructions.

From today, food should no longer be labelled as good or bad, she told us. There should be no more talk about diets and health food in our household, because eating-disorder patients disguised their avoidance of sugary and fatty foods by pretending to eat clean.

"Sure," I uttered, to let Sally know that she could count on us, but at the same time I thought how ridiculous it was that we suddenly had to think of doughnuts as nourishment. What was wrong with swapping a cheeseburger for a Buddha bowl? I had encouraged that, but I could sense that it was pointless to discuss my beliefs with her. I tugged at my hair and stared at the floor.

Lastly, Sally explained to us the difference between cognitive-behavioural therapy for eating disorders and family-based therapy for adolescents. I don't recall much of the conversation, only that we decided to go ahead with family-based therapy.

"Here's the thing," she said, looking directly at Fiona. "Family-based therapy means that Mum and Dad will decide when, what, and how much you'll eat. I know this will be extremely difficult for you to accept, because as a teenager you want to be in control. The last thing you want is your parents telling you what to do. Please understand that this is only temporary and that you can still be in charge in other areas of your life."

I cast a quick glance at Fiona. Her face was turning pale.

"At the moment, your eating-disorder voice wants to be in charge of what you eat. Starting tomorrow, your parents will be," she told her.

Then Sally changed her tone of voice to a more assertive one, and she looked at all of us as she explained, "What you have to understand is that Fiona has little control over her illness. Her malnourished brain is not thinking rationally. Therefore, the first thing that we have to do is to teach Fiona's brain that she'll never make herself starve again, and we'll do that by making her eat regularly. Gradually, her brain will stop obsessing about food."

That was what she had said, and that was what I had heard, but for some reason my mind was clouded and didn't process the information properly. Perhaps because Fiona didn't look malnourished to me.

"Fiona," the therapist continued, "this will be the hardest thing that you'll ever have to do in your life."

I looked sideways and saw my brave girl fighting her terror and tears. I squeezed her delicate hand, as if to say, *you can do this, sweetheart.*

Then the therapist turned her head ever so slightly to look at just Tom and me and she said, "And this will be the hardest thing that *you* will ever have to do in *your* life. You'll have to support each other, because even the slightest disagreement between the two of you will put the eating disorder back in charge. Do you understand?"

Out of the corner of my eye, I saw tears in Tom's eyes. It made me realise how vulnerable and worn out we all were. He blinked rapidly so that the tears would go away unnoticed, just like he always did when he watched a sad movie. We nodded and obediently bowed our heads like at the end of a sermon. We were handing over Fiona's future to Sally. We had to trust her.

That night I woke up at two o'clock and laid awake for a while. I rolled on my side, closed my eyes, and considered how fortunate we were to finally have a plan. Five months we had waited for this to happen. It was going to cost us a fortune, but we could afford it. I had heard of people selling their houses in order to pay for therapy.

And wasn't it a remarkable concurrence that at the stroke of midnight, New Zealand had moved to COVID-19 Alert Level Four? This meant that we were summoned to stay wherever we were and form a bubble with the people we happened to be with at the time. How ideal that we had the opportunity to feed Fiona without her having to miss school! I felt a rush of gratitude fill my body which gave way to nonsensical excitement. If only Gordon Ramsey

CHAPTER 3

could be in our bubble! Effortlessly he would whip up three well-balanced meals a day with two snacks in between and another snack after dinner, in exact three-hour intervals.

Tom cooked occasionally, on Saturdays. He would prepare spaghetti Bolognese with raw spinach leaves out of a bag to the side and Paul Newman's salad dressing, or he would serve us "Tom's stir fry," which consisted of vegetables and shrimp thrown together in a wok and garnished with little hills of dill.

I only loved cooking in theory, and I had secretly hoped that lockdown would give me the perfect excuse to cook simple and boring meals for weeks, but Sally had changed the game plan. *I shouldn't let myself get worked up about the meal planning,* I told myself. I was so pleased Fiona liked Sally. That was most important. I gently drifted back to sleep.

A rustling noise ripped me out of my dream. It had been a hot night, and we had slept with our bedroom doors wide open. *The rustling must be Fiona's duvet,* I thought. It didn't stop. She was restless. I checked my alarm. It was only six o'clock. For the last ten weeks, Fiona had been waking up so incredibly early. Hunger was messing with her teenage circadian rhythm. I wasn't a morning person, but I shot out of bed, fired up to begin our first day of family-based therapy. I threw my bathrobe over my singlet and boxers and ran downstairs.

Ordinarily, we would start the day with a chilled help-yourself breakfast. Today was going to be different. I tried to predict what Fiona might like to eat, scrambled two eggs, threw a slice of bread in the toaster, and poured a glass of milk.

"I'm dairy intolerant. Did you forget?" Fiona's voice snapped. I hadn't noticed her sneaking up behind me.

"Oh, good morning," I chirped and turned around to give her a hug, but she walked away from me in her baggy T-shirt and silky pyjama shorts.

Sheepishly I poured the milk down the drain.

"Tea?"

"A green one." She sat down at the kitchen table. "Why are you putting butter on my toast!?" she shouted.

Oh, boy.

"By the way, butter is dairy, too," she lectured me.

Quietly I scraped the butter off the toast and spread jam on it. I filled a bowl with yoghurt and granola for myself, joined her at the table and ate. Small talk was difficult with the eating disorder on both of our minds and not much else happening. I sensed how stressed she was.

"What am I going to do all day?" she asked.

"You could watch a movie," I said. "I have to pick apples later. You could help."

"I'm not picking apples." Fiona stuck her lip out.

Tom came downstairs to grab a croissant. I asked him to go to the supermarket before the queues got too long.

"I'll write you a list," I said. "And don't forget your mask."

After Tom had left, I had about an hour and a half until snack time. I cleaned the fridge, threw a load of laundry in the washing machine, and vacuumed the house. At five to nine, I noticed that Fiona was already sitting at the kitchen table waiting. She had neither showered nor changed out of her nightclothes. Curled up on her unmade bed, she had waited for the time to pass until her next feed. I placed two apples and two muesli bars on the table.

"I'll eat the apple, but I don't want the muesli bar," Fiona said quickly. "I'm not that hungry because I haven't done anything all day."

"I hear you."

I was still full myself, and I had to force the apple down my throat, but I felt that I needed to accompany her and eat same-sized meals, because I knew that Fiona thought of me as skinny. That I lacked the untamed metabolism of a growing teenager at my age was irrelevant to Fiona. Eating a smaller amount than her would have made her feel fat and greedy. It was that simple. I unwrapped the muesli bar and looked at her, hoping to earn a smile. She had her head down and stared at her phone while she grazed on the apple.

"Fiona, could you please not be on your phone while you eat?"

"Why?"

Without warning, the front door flew open. Tom rushed into the kitchen. He plopped four grocery bags on the kitchen counter. Packets of pasta fell on the floor. He joked about the supermarket queue. "Felt like being back in

CHAPTER 3

South Carolina with a hurricane coming," he said.

"Yup, I can imagine," I said and laughed. "Fiona, do you remember those days? You were only twelve years old when Hurricane Joaquin hit. We had to board up our windows. Then we lost electricity. You were so happy that everybody was at home, and you twirled around the house."

"Mum, just don't. Can I get up now?"

She hadn't touched the muesli bar. I didn't know what to do. I looked at the clock.

"In fifteen minutes, darling."

When Fiona was back in her bedroom, I made a cup of coffee and sat back down again. It was barely ten o'clock. Beset with doubts, I thought about her breakfast comment. *Why did she say that she is lactose intolerant? I'm the only one in the family whose stomach hurts after drinking milk.* I also wondered if I should have insisted on her eating the muesli bar or whether the apple had been enough.

Sally hadn't mentioned anything about calories, and I hadn't asked, because I didn't want her to know that I had no clue how many calories were in a scoop of ice cream. The truth was, I didn't care. Calorie counting was scientifically flawed and a waste of time. The fact that I consumed double the amount of what Tom ate, but yet I happened to be the skinnier of the two of us, seemed to prove me right. When the kids were younger, I had been interested in nutritional healing, and somewhere I had read that the burning of calories is a complex and individualised process. Sleep, stress, and liver function, among other things, influence how our bodies burn calories. The caloric value on a food label is a mere estimate, with the margin of error sometimes as high as twenty percent. Not only that, but food preparation also plays its part, with the caloric intake from a raw tomato being different from that of a fried tomato. It baffled me that diet advocates, gym gurus, and sadly my own daughter counted calories religiously.

Having said that, without being able to rely on calories as a measurement, I was confused about how much to feed our malnourished teenager. Sally had said that we should serve Fiona a reasonable amount. *Maybe I should email her and ask her to be more specific,* I thought, but then I never did. Tired of thinking about food, I topped up my coffee and walked outside to get some fresh air and to see how far Tom had gotten with the conversion of our "hippie bus."

The dark blue Toyota HiAce was sitting in the middle of the driveway, doors wide open. I saw Tom kneeling behind the passenger seat. For the last week, he had been busy building the double bed. Today he was installing the sink. I hopped inside the van and sat on the mattress. With my feet dangling down, I watched him for a while.

Tom was such a practical man, but he wasn't a good listener. He disassociated, never got involved with heart and soul, and although I knew that deep inside he cared for me, with time it had become harder and harder to love him. But I wasn't giving myself permission to separate and break up our family. Tom acted as if everything was still as it should be between a middle-aged wife and husband. We had talked about the lack of connection in our relationship many times, but then we continued to ignore the cracks, maybe out of convenience, who knows. For the moment, it was important that we focused on Fiona's recovery.

"I think I'll make tuna sandwiches for lunch."

"Fine with me," he said.

Eric opened the sliding door of his apartment and stuck his head out.

"Good morning, amigo!" I called.

He smiled. "Where's Fiona?"

"In her room, on her phone. Come on, Eric, let's go to the orchard and pick apples."

When we got back to the house, it was time for lunch.

"Mum, I don't eat tuna. It's fish!" Fiona protested. "You actually have to serve me food that I eat. You know that, don't you?"

Since when was she vegetarian? I guess a few months ago, she had mentioned something about poor animals and the neighbour's daughter Alicia not eating meat, but I hadn't taken it seriously because she still ate chicken and salmon. *Perhaps she only feels sorry for certain animals, the dead tuna being one of them. Or is it that she thinks the added mayonnaise will make her fat and she's deceiving me?*

CHAPTER 3

"I'm sorry, Fiona, but that's what we're having."

"I'm not eating tuna," she repeated.

My hands closed into fists as I stood with my back to her at the kitchen counter. She was sitting at the table, and I heard her push her plate across it. She was testing me.

"What's Dad having for lunch?" she asked.

"Tuna sandwiches," I said while I opened the fridge. "I could make you a cheese sandwich instead," I offered.

"No, thanks."

"You'll have to eat something, Fiona."

"Okay, I'll eat the tuna then," she said and pulled the plate close.

Hopeful, I sat down opposite her, nibbling at my own sandwich. It tasted of nothing.

Feeding a teenager requires a different mindset than feeding a toddler. Years back, when two-year-old Fiona would refuse to eat her vegetables, her spoon would magically transform into a noisy cargo plane with broccoli on board. The plane would take off from her plate, circle the air, and safely land in her mouth. For as long as we played the game, she happily sat on my lap, ate, and giggled. Unfortunately, it was impossible to revive the innocent game and the old stamina. But what else could I do?

Sit with her and distract her, the therapist had said. The eating disorder voice is very loud when she eats. So I'd better sit with her and eat, even if I'm not hungry.

"How is your friend Eva?" I asked.

"You've already asked me that this morning. Are you losing it?"

"Sorry. I meant to say, what's she up to during lockdown?"

"What do you think? She's on her phone. Everyone is on their phones."

"Dad is doing a fabulous job with the 'hippie bus.'"

"It's not a bus, Mum, it's a van. You're always using the wrong words. Honestly, I think your English is getting worse as you get older."

"Whatever it is, you should have a look."

"When I get back from my walk," she said.

"Do you want to go on your own?"

"Yes."

"All right. I'll let you go in twenty minutes."

I was surprised that Fiona accepted the afternoon snack without resistance. At dinner, after I had dished out medium-sized portions of vegetable lasagne for everyone, I caught myself staring at Fiona. Over the last months, I had become obsessed with evaluating the way she ate and tried to interpret her facial expressions. Tonight, she ate slowly and declined a second serving.

"How about two small packs of chocolate-chip cookies?" I knew it was a mistake to ask her what she wanted to have for her evening snack.

Agitated, she opened the pantry door and began to search for something different, but she couldn't find anything that she liked. "You really need to go shopping!" she shouted.

That was when I caught myself screaming at her inside my head.

Millions of kids on this planet have nothing to eat but a bowl of rice, and she wants choices. This isn't a restaurant. If she honestly wants to heal, she'd better shut up and eat what I give her!

I observed her rip an oat bar out of an opened package of six. We sat down on the sofa, side by side, without speaking. I put my elbows on my knees and placed my head in my hands. I missed my Fiona, the kind and cheeky one. While she was munching on the oat bar, I wanted to ask her how she was doing, but I didn't. I was too scared. She had calmed down, and I wanted to leave it at that.

She said she was tired. I realised that the day had been long for her, and cruel. I stroked her hair until she was allowed to get up to shower, which was twenty minutes after her last bite of food. Then I wandered upstairs, entered the master bedroom, and sat on the end of my side of the bed. Tom was resting with his head propped up on a pillow whilst reading the news on his phone.

"What's happening?" he inquired without looking up.

"I'm exhausted," I told him.

"From what?" he asked, smiling at me. It was frustrating how he seemed to live on a different planet.

"From dealing with Fiona. It's hard."

CHAPTER 3

"It's only been one day."

"I know."

"Well, don't argue with her, and do what Sally has said."

"Could you do one of the meals tomorrow, please?" I asked.

"No worries, I'll make her lunch."

The following day, half an hour after the mid-morning snack, I walked to my favourite spot in the garden. It was an oval-shaped clearing. Surrounded by nikau palm trees and copper-coloured grasses, it was the lowest area of our one-hectare (about 2.5 acres) large property. In winter, a large part of it would turn into a small pond, but during the dry months, two Cape Cod chairs lived underneath the palms. Our house wasn't visible from the clearing, and as long as the neighbour's dog hadn't detected my scent, I could sit here in silence and pretend I was somewhere else. I had taken a book with me, but it stayed unopened. Instead, I listened to the buzzing of the bees and thought of nothing until lunchtime was coming up.

I was apprehensive about Tom looking after Fiona and slowly strolled back to the house. As I came closer, I heard her shouting. My heart sank. When I entered the house, I wasn't surprised to see Fiona all alone in front of a ham-and-cheese sandwich that looked like it was soaked with tears. Tom had settled in one of the armchairs at the other end of the room. He was texting someone.

"What's going on?" I asked.

Tom explained that he was going to shut the modem off if Fiona wasn't eating her lunch. He had an all-or-nothing approach to parenting that I distinctly disliked.

"Mum, if Dad is shutting the Wi-Fi off, I'm moving out," she shouted.

"Lower your voice, Fiona, please," I said. "Now, eat your sandwich, then all will be good. I'll sit with you."

"I don't eat ham. Dad knows that. He can't force me to eat something that will make me sick!"

Tom had enough. He jumped up from his seat, walked into the hallway and took the modem off the shelf.

Fiona ran into her room and slammed the door.

"Tom, this doesn't work," I implored. "We need to sit with her while she's eating. And you can't be on your phone. Switch the Wi-Fi back on, this is ridiculous."

Tom responded in a way men often do when discussing a serious issue that feels like too much trouble. "I can never do anything right," he said and rushed out of the house.

I called Fiona and prepared an alternative lunch. We ate avocado sandwiches and drank freshly pressed orange juice. Both of us were silent.

Halfway through lunch, she looked up at me and smiled slightly. She felt safe again, and I did too. Both of us had given in to our inner voices and their foolish excuses. Suddenly, contempt for the manipulative person that she had become shot up my throat like acid reflux. Her behaviour made me feel powerless and angry, but giving in to those feelings would not have seemed right, either.

After lunch, I decided to spend a couple of hours with Eric. I entered his apartment with the intention to talk with him about his new job, but instead I collapsed on his couch and fell asleep within minutes. When I woke up, it was half an hour past afternoon snack time. I ran upstairs, grabbed two bananas, and flew into Fiona's bedroom. She was in a good mood. She had talked to Anthony for the last two hours. They had made arrangements for him to come over tomorrow and stay with us for a week or two.

"Fiona, I don't think this is a good idea. Anthony has his sisters from Wellington staying with him, and we don't know if they have caught COVID. They probably haven't, but he should not leave his bubble. I'm sure Anthony's parents won't let him come to us anyways."

"No, Mum, they're fine with it," she said confidently.

"Yes, but I'm not. He can come over when we move to Alert Level Three."

"Why are you so uptight all of a sudden?"

"Fiona, it's *illegal* to have him come over. We could get fined."

"Since when do you care about that?"

"Since today," I said, threw a banana on her bed, and left her room. Something smashed.

CHAPTER 3

I heard Fiona scream how horrible I was and how much she hated me.

I tried my best to ignore her and walked into the lounge. Her bedroom door slammed, then the front door.

From the balcony, I could see her running down the driveway, barefoot, in her tent-like T-shirt and shorts. I was in a cold sweat. The boat ramp was close enough for teenage impulsivity to drown her within minutes. Where the hell was Tom? I searched for my car keys. Tom appeared, and I ordered him to drive around the neighbourhood.

I emailed Sally.

To my surprise, she responded instantly. "Don't hesitate to contact the police," she wrote.

I was shocked. *The last thing I want to do is call the police on my own daughter!* I hesitated. It would take her three hours to walk to Anthony's. I marched back and forth between the house and the letterbox, praying for Fiona to come back.

When she did, after about an hour or so, I followed her into her room. She seemed absent. Her body looked hollow and sad. The banana laid untouched on the bed. I watched her shut her curtains and sit on the bed with her back to me. I realised how unpredictable and manipulative her behaviour was, and then again, I knew it was the illness and not her. She suffered, and my identification with her suffering had made me hypersensitive and afraid to put my foot down. I didn't want to cause further suffering. I just wanted her to be at peace.

She needed Anthony. He would distract her from her own relentless inner critic. And so, I softly touched her shoulder with the tips of my fingers and whispered, "All right, call Tony. He's allowed to come over."

During our second therapy session, we had to eat a meal in front of the laptop screen. Sally pointed out that Fiona ate with a teaspoon.

"I'd like you to use a tablespoon like everyone else," she told Fiona. Then she looked at Tom and inquired about the first week of therapy. He said that things had been going fine. I disagreed.

"I'm struggling, Sally," I said. "When Fiona says she's not hungry, I don't know what to do, because I myself would hate to be forced to eat when feeling full."

"What if Fiona were sick with cancer and she didn't like the treatment? Would you stop giving her the medication?" she asked. "Bulimia can *kill*. Food is medicine. Fiona is your patient. She doesn't decide. You decide what to give her and how much."

I made every effort to stay firm. But again and again, Fiona challenged me. And I couldn't bear to see her pain. It was easy for the eating disorder to take advantage of both of us. And so, when Fiona said that scrambled eggs three times in a row were unacceptable, and when she said that I couldn't expect her to clean her plate when her stomach was bloated and hard, I gave in.

And each time I would remember the cancer analogy and feel like a failure.

"We have no choices for snacks," Fiona complained to Sally in one of the sessions. "And by the way, Mum's cooking isn't the greatest."

Sally threw me a questioning look. Embarrassed, I defended myself saying that I had planned to buy a large plastic container and to fill it with packs of pretzels, strawberry fruit strings, crisps, popcorn, and various muesli bars.

"I even have a name for it. We'll call it The Snack Box," I said. "Nobody will be allowed to touch it but Fiona."

"Hold on a minute," Sally said. "*You're* the one picking the snack out of the box, not Fiona. We don't want her to be comparing the calories of popcorn with crisps and then try to get away with the snack with the least amount of calories. The eating disorder is not allowed to make any decisions."

My evenings were much the same in the ten months that followed. After the last snack of the day, I would go upstairs, my movements slow as if I had suddenly aged by many years. I would switch on the table lamp with the soft light and take a seat on the sofa. Strained from the battle against Fiona's bulimia voice, I would lean my head back, and tears would wet my face. I would stay awake until I was sure Fiona was fast asleep, because sometimes when overcome by a crazy hunger, she would get up again and check if my light was still on. The light which indicated that I was awake protected her from binge eating in secret.

CHAPTER 3

One night, she called my name because she still wanted a yoghurt. I came downstairs to sit with her. When she had finished, I put her to bed and wrapped her tight into her blanket because she was freezing. I put my hands on her shoulders to hug her.

She shuddered. "Don't touch me."

"Okay. Sleep well, Poppy," I answered and left her room.

Much later I was startled by the creak of her bedroom door.

"Fiona?"

"Yes," she whispered.

"Come upstairs. I'm still awake."

She raced to the upper level and plummeted next to me on the sofa.

"I can't fall sleep," she said.

"I know," I nodded. "That's okay."

She snuggled up tight placing her head on my lap. I rested my warm hands on her back and shoulder. Suddenly, it felt as if the bulimia voice had finally shut its gob, not in defeat, just momentarily intimidated by something greater.

"We'll get there," I said to reassure us both, and she looked up at me with hopeful eyes. "I promise."

Chapter 4

When I learned that my daughter's body and brain were that of a famine victim, I cried because of the tragedy of it all. She felt cold in the midst of summer. She was extremely irritable. Even the littlest things annoyed her. Although she was still able to solve mental problems, her motivation to do so had diminished.

The only thing Fiona thought about was food.

She stared at images of online dishes and watched people eat impressive meals. She suffered from depressive mood, apathy, and loss of judgment.

She had adopted strange rituals when eating her meals. Often, she cut her food into tiny pieces and took hours to eat. *Exactly* like the men that took part in the Minnesota Starvation Experiment, an experiment conducted in 1944 with the intention to gather empirical knowledge to assist with the rehabilitation of famine victims at the end of WWII.

Thirty-six healthy and stable men had been semi-starved for several months. The changes in the men's physical and mental health during the starvation period and during rehabilitation bore such a striking resemblance to what I observed in Fiona, it sent shivers up my spine. Four men broke the diet, only to start binge eating. After the re-feeding program was completed, some men were unable to understand their hunger cues for months afterwards. Their minds constantly feared that food could become scarce again. As a result, their hunger became insatiable.

It made perfect sense that this experiment was mentioned by psychologists in the context of eating disorders. There was no difference between extreme dieting and starvation. But why had nobody shown us the video? Health

CHAPTER 4

nurses, GP, psychiatrist, therapist, nobody had mentioned anything. Perhaps they didn't know it existed. I had to find it myself this morning. I pushed my laptop across the table and wiped the tears off my face. At any moment, Fiona could come into the kitchen, and I didn't want her to see me upset.

I decided to tell Tom about the video later that night. He had gone downstairs to his tool shed. I could hear him whistling. He had said that he wanted to fix the two broken boards on the deck in front of Eric's apartment. *But it's only eight in the morning*, I thought. *He should have waited to use the table saw until Eric was awake.* I laid my head down on my arms. I was glad the video had demystified why Fiona was so irrational and unresponsive at times. I could see now why Sally had said that Fiona had no control. I felt foolish. Why hadn't I gotten it straight away? I needed to make up for it with determination.

During the weeks that followed, I placed meal after meal in front of Fiona without allowing the manipulative comments of the bulimia voice to trick my emotions. When she stood behind me one lunchtime and demanded that we eat cauliflower instead of basmati rice, I spun around and sent her out of the kitchen. And when on another day she refused to eat pancakes with maple syrup for breakfast, I picked up the phone and threatened to call Sally. And when she claimed that her stomach ached and that there was no way that she could swallow another bite of her dinner, I bluffed, warning her that I had Sally's private number and wouldn't hesitate to phone her at home. While I fed her malnourished body, I suspected that the eating-disorder voice roared inside her head like a wild cat and dug its claws deeply into her self-worth, because she never opened her bedroom curtains anymore.

Then one morning, I overheard her ripping coat hangers off the wardrobe rail. I was unloading the dishwasher. I called her for her morning snack; she wouldn't come. I knocked on her door.

"Fiona? What's going on?"

"I'm selling my clothes on Depop," she proclaimed triumphantly, "because they don't fit. I hate them."

I entered her bedroom. T-shirts, jeans, shorts, dresses, and swimwear lay scattered on the ground, ready to be rolled up and shipped out. My eyes scanned the inside of her large built-in wardrobe. The only items I could still see hanging up were two lonely T-shirts and her school uniform.

"Fiona, we don't have the money to buy you a whole heap of new outfits. You'll hardly get anything for your clothes on this De-thing. What did you say it was called?"

"Depop."

I bent down to pick up a gorgeous corduroy jacket. We had ordered it from Australia barely eight months ago.

"You can't sell this!"

"I'm selling it."

"Fiona, please."

"Too late, Mum, somebody's actually already bought it."

I was boiling inside. I knew if she told me the sale price, I would lose my shit. So, I didn't ask.

"Nice clothes are expensive," I said, but she just shrugged her shoulders. And then she said that she didn't care.

A few days after her clothes had disappeared, she had a meltdown because she didn't know what to wear. I hugged her tenderly and I promised that I would dip into my savings and that we would order brand-new ones. Clothes that would make her feel more comfortable. I forgave her.

But when it came to mealtimes, I remained stubborn and firm.

And she ate.

It must have been late April. I had finished cleaning the kitchen and stood in the lounge checking my phone for no reason when Fiona came out of her bedroom holding a thin book in her hands. It was a novel that she had been asked to read for English class, she said.

"What's the name of it?"

"The Great Gatsby." On the verge of tears, she declared that she had been trying to concentrate on the words, but she had found it too hard to read on her own.

"I could read to you like I did in the olden days when you were a little girl. Remember that?"

CHAPTER 4

"Yes," she sniffled, "I'd love that."

"All right, let's get comfortable then."

I opened the sliding doors to the balcony. Light yellow sun rays and the noisy offbeat sound of a tui bird penetrated our serious lounge. She handed me the book and I hunkered down in the green armchair. Fiona went to lie down on the sofa with her head on a cushion and her feet propped up on the armrest. She tucked her phone behind her back, and I began to read.

And that's what it would be like for the next ten days, every afternoon at three. Fiona would remember precisely where we had left off the day before. The story gave us temporary relief from our demanding realities, as we tiptoed in our minds into the social circles of insanely wealthy Americans. We entered Gatsby's lit-up mansion, joined his parties, and watched the rich get drunk and live out their envy, pride, and lust. We witnessed the American Dream gone hysterical. *Nothing has changed much*, I thought to myself. A hundred years had passed since the novel was written, but we were still neurotic. Or worse perhaps. Trying to achieve perfect looks that normalised eating-disorder behaviours.

I enjoyed reading to Fiona. For once, I wasn't scrambling around for eating-disorder-friendly small talk.

After we finished the novel, we watched the movie. Fiona dragged her quilted baby blanket into the Netflix room. The colours of the blanket had faded, and she had clearly outgrown it in size, but it offered security, and it hid parts of her body. I was still sorting through the pantry when she slid into the recliner chair and grabbed the remote. With both feet, she moved the chair backwards, rolled up one corner of the blanket, and rested her head on it.

"I'm starting the movie," she yelled.

I arrived with two bowls of pretzels and placed them on the bamboo table in between her chair and the three-seater couch where I was going to sit.

"I love *The Great Gatsby*," she told me. "Nick is my favourite character. Do you want to know why?" She threw me a questioning look. "He doesn't judge."

"Interesting you say that," I replied.

"Even though he's the one telling us the story, he isn't moralistic. Have you not noticed?"

To be fair, I hadn't really paid much attention to Nick's role, but I could immediately see why she had. Being highly sensitive, Fiona easily picked up on subtleties. Her brain registered and interpreted the tiniest of gestures and the quietest of remarks, and then she remembered them forever. She could read body language and tone of voice better than most. But with her sensitivity came an undesirably high level of self-awareness. She hated that people would constantly judge her and others.

Every so often while the movie played, I glanced at her face. She had her mouth slightly open, and her eyes fixed on the TV. I took immense pleasure in seeing her distracted from her pain. When the credentials rolled over the screen, we turned to each other and agreed that we preferred the book to the movie. And then we were quiet for a few long moments, and content, as if we had achieved something.

"To tell you the truth, Mum, I wish they would've warned us." The rage in her voice ripped me out of my meditative state.

I had no idea what she was referring to.

"When I was in Year Eleven, I didn't know that dieting can lead to an eating disorder. If I'd known, I would've never thrown my lunches in the bin. Never. But no teacher ever said anything."

I turned my head to look at her. She still appeared relaxed with her head tilted to one side resting on the blanket, but I knew she wasn't. Underneath her oversized T-shirt was a hungry, worn-out body. Her words had come from the depths of her heart. And she was right. Bulimia was set into motion by dieting. No matter what the other underlying causes might be, without food restriction, there would be no binge eating and no purging.

"Every year," Fiona continued, "we have to sit through endless talks about drugs. These people come into assembly, and they warn us about meth and all sorts of other stuff, but they never say a fucking thing about dieting."

It was out of character for Fiona to swear like that. I understood why she was angry. *If only the school had invited someone who had recovered from an eating disorder as a guest speaker, or if at least one of the teachers would have* been bothered enough to make a short presentation about the correlation between dieting and eating disorders, this ugly, painful mess that she was in could perhaps have been prevented.* It was excruciating to hear my own thoughts.

"You know, Fiona," I began, feeling unpleasantly exhausted, "in all those years that I was teaching in Christchurch, we never discussed eating disorders in the staff room. It wasn't on our agenda. We talked about racial discrimination, abuse, and drugs, of course, but dieting, no. It's so sad, come to think of it."

"It needs to change," she said.

"Yes, you're right."

I stood up, approached the recliner chair and gently kissed her on the head. I had some good news to share with her that I had purposely saved for after the movie.

"Guess what, Fiona? This morning I received an email letter from the dog breeder. The letter allows me to cross the regional checkpoints. I can finally go and pick up the puppy."

"Yay! I've been waiting for that!" Fiona shot upright. She smiled at me.

"Well, have you thought of a name yet?" I asked.

"I was thinking of Teddy, or maybe Winston. What do you think?"

"I like Winston better."

"I agree. Winston will suit him, and it's not so common. Oh, I'm so excited!"

"We're very lucky to get a brown labradoodle. You know that, don't you?"

"Yes, I do. Oohhh, I can't wait now. Will Winston be allowed to sleep on my bed?"

"Of course."

Only four days later, the fluffy Winston arrived, looking more like a teddy bear than a dog, as he sat on Fiona's bed. She threw her arms around him, smiled, and patted his head.

I knelt in front of the bed, looked into his calm dark eyes and spoke to him in my thoughts. *My darling pup, I have a pretty difficult job for you to do, but I can already tell by your temperament that you're up for it. See this little girl next to you? She doesn't trust herself anymore, but I know she'll trust you. Show her your unconditional love and affection. You'll be able to make a difference in her life.*

During Winston's first weeks with us, he thought of Fiona as his master. She taught him tricks, took him for walks, made him jump over stone walls, threw sticks for him, and fed him. Every day she reminded us how smart he was, and how adorable he looked on all the Instagram photos she had taken of him.

But then the novelty wore off, and her occupation with food gained ground on Winston.

Eventually, I became Winston's master and had to put up with slobbery dog kisses, fur, and wet mud prints on the white tiles in the hallway. But I did gladly because Winston never let anyone down. Eric also benefited from his company. Both enjoyed playing hide-and-seek in the garden.

On tough days when Fiona was feeling fat and wouldn't allow anyone to touch her, Winston was the only one given permission to snuggle up to her, and she would fall asleep with her head on his woolly back. After a while, he would get hot and feel uncomfortable, but he wouldn't dare move.

Puppies quickly become the talk of the neighbourhood, and so one afternoon, our friends David, Elena, and their daughter Alicia, who lived only a two-minute drive from us, stopped by for a visit, curious to meet Winston and eager to get a break from life in isolation. I was glad Anthony had left this morning because we had hidden from everybody that he'd been coming in and out of our bubble. I already knew the neighbours were coming before I saw them, because David had a voice and a laughter that would echo through the entire neighbourhood. He was a short British man with a ponytail, a few years younger than Tom and me. When he arrived, he told us that for the last few weeks, he had been drinking every single day. According to him, this was an ideal way to hibernate during lockdown. I faked a smile while Tom chuckled and led the way to our van. David followed, keeping his two-meter distance. Tom opened the back to demonstrate the mechanics of the ingenious pull-out kitchen area that he had built. Alicia, who was the same age as Fiona, took a seat near her on the stairs leading up to the house. She patted Winston and looked at her mother in a way that prompted Elena to say, "No, Alicia, we're not getting a dog."

Elena asked me if I wanted to go for a walk around the property. She was

CHAPTER 4

always keen to look at my plantings.

"I haven't done much lately," I said but she didn't hear me.

I liked Elena. She was a redhead who was always full of inspiring ideas. One year, she had forced everyone in her family to sign up for a pottery course. The following year, she enrolled them in Tai Chi classes and tried herself at competitive yo-yoing. Therefore, I was surprised on this day when I noticed that her bubbly nature had deflated. She even looked depressed.

Halfway down the driveway, she stopped in her steps and sat down on a large volcanic rock. She wanted to talk to me away from everybody else. Asking her how she had been coping with the lockdown made me realise how much I myself yearned for someone to listen to my story.

"It truly has been a nightmare," she sighed. "Alicia gets so frustrated with these Zoom lessons. She's got it in her head now that she's fallen behind."

"Oh, she shouldn't. I'm sure teachers will repeat much of the lessons' content once school starts back up again," I said.

"That's what I keep telling her, but she doesn't want to listen. She's so stressed, and she's making our lives miserable. I don't know what to do with her. All day she's on her stupid phone. She doesn't want to do anything else. She used to love reading books and doing art. One picture she's painted so far. One. And she's grumpy because she's not allowed see her friends. This living in isolation is so difficult for teenagers."

I wanted to give Elena a hug but then I remembered that I wasn't allowed to.

"I agree," I said in a sympathetic voice. "They feel that they're missing out on so much. But case numbers have lowered. I'm confident that things will change soon."

"And she's constantly hungry, you know. Teenagers! They just eat all the time. Then she bakes and leaves the unwashed bowls and trays all over the counters expecting me to clean up after her. I'm fed up, honestly."

She sort of laughed. I stared at the ground. I was tempted to say that I wished Fiona would bake and eat cakes. I would be more than prepared to do the dishes.

"You're right," she continued without waiting for me to say something.

"Soon the kids will be back in school, we'll be at work, and everything will be fine. We'll just have to hang in there for another week or so and support each other. How's Fiona? Is she coping?"

"Actually, she enjoys the Zoom lessons. Yeah, she's not doing too badly. I guess I'm lucky," I told her.

Not long after the neighbour friends' visit, Tom shaved his beard off and announced that he would go back to work to prepare for Alert Level Two. He had de-stressed while in lockdown, and his natural nervousness had subsided to such a degree that he had picked up drinking chamomile tea. He was pleased with himself because the camper was finished and everybody in the family had said something nice about it.

It was on the night when we had lemon chicken and potato salad that I wondered how much of what was going on around him he actually took in. Fiona and Eric were already sitting at the table, and I was spooning the potato salad on everybody's plate, when Tom came flying through the front door. He greeted us with *howdy*, slammed his car keys and phone on the sideboard in the lounge and joined us at the table.

"Where is Winston?" he asked, searching the room with his eyes.

"In my room," Fiona said, "coz we don't want him to beg."

Tom leaned back, slapped his protruding belly with both hands and announced, "I haven't eaten anything all day. I'm getting fat, I ..."

"Ahem ... Tom," I interrupted while squinting at Fiona.

She had her head down, which made it impossible for me to see her facial reaction. I hoped that she hadn't heard what he had said, but that was of course absurd. Tom sat right next to her.

"How was work?" I asked.

Tom uttered something about his boss being an idiot, pecked at a small bowl of potato salad, got up, and left to watch TV. I put my knife and fork down and plucked on the skin around my nails. *I can't let myself get worked up about Tom's small ignorant comments*, I thought, but my appetite had vanished. I was glad when Eric interrupted the silence. He told us that the police had stopped him last night when he came home from work.

"I showed the officer the letter that I have in my car and told him that I'm an essential worker."

"Well done," I said, doing my best to sound cheerful. "You're the man. You keep the nation going."

"You're exaggerating as usual," he commented in his deep voice, but he smiled proudly.

"Don't bring those COVID germs home," Fiona piped.

"Na, I won't. I always soap my hands after work, not like you, Mother," he said, and crinkles formed around his eyes. "You never soap your hands when you come home from shopping."

"He's right," Fiona said.

We quietly finished our dinner. Then I asked Eric to stay at the table with us for a wee while. He suggested a round of chess, but Fiona and I were not in the mood.

"You'll whip us anyway," she said.

Later that evening when I walked into Fiona's room to bring her a snack, she pulled on my arm, begging for me to sit next to her on the bed.

"I don't want Dad to be part of the therapy anymore," she said. "And I mean it."

"Why is that?"

"Cos Dad doesn't understand. Did you not hear him at dinner?"

"Yes, I did."

"And last week he said something about eating spinach leaves for lunch."

"Did he?" I pretended that I hadn't heard him.

"Yes, Mum, he's done this a few times. You need to talk to him. He can't say those things around me."

"I've talked to him already. He forgets. But I'll remind him again," I promised.

"He's so embarrassing in the therapy sessions."

"Yes, all right. We'll talk with Sally, but she might insist that he continues to take part. He needs to hear how we as parents can support you."

"You can tell him."

"It's not the same."

"Mum, please."

"Okay, okay," I said. "I'll email Sally."

That night, before Tom switched off his phone and the bedside lamp to go to sleep, I sat on his side of the bed, my thigh touching his feet. It had become a routine that I would give him an account of Fiona's emotional condition at least twice a week. He would listen but rarely say a word in return. Tonight I brought up Fiona's request, unsure how he would take it.

"Why?" he asked.

I thought carefully about what to say next.

"Er ... she feels uncomfortable."

"To hell then. I don't need to take part. Sally isn't telling us anything new anyway. She just repeats herself."

"She does and she doesn't," I said defensively because I had gained strength when I realised that he hadn't taken Fiona's wish too personally. "You have to admit that she does it because most of the time we aren't getting it."

"I'd disagree. Anyway, I find early afternoons difficult to make because of work, so you might as well tell me what's been said in the sessions."

For him the conversation had ended.

"Mm-hmm," I said. "There's one more thing. Could you please be mindful of what you say when Fiona is around? You can't be talking about not eating all day, because that's exactly what the eating disorder voice wants her to do. I have told you that before."

"The whole world talks about dieting," he said, a little angry now. "It's not just me. She needs to get used to it and learn to harden up. A small comment here and there can't hurt."

His reaction struck a raw nerve, because I felt guilty of thinking the same in moments when I was struggling with exhaustion—but I didn't want Tom to say these kinds of things out loud.

"She has a mental illness, Tom."

"All right, I'll keep my mouth shut."

"Please, don't be like that." I got up and left the room. Then I closed the door shut behind me. I was always explaining the same things, and I was sick of it. Standing on the landing, not knowing what to do next, I noticed that I had become a lot like Fiona. Exhausted, absent-minded, and indecisive.

Tired, I sat down on the carpet, pulled my yoga mat out from underneath the sofa, knelt on it, bent forward, and stretched into child's pose. With my forehead resting on the mat, I tried to reboot life, marriage, motherhood. Everything.

I asked myself: *Why didn't I marry a tall man with a muscular chest I can lean my head against? That's all I want. It can be so simple.* Not that being married to Tom was complicated. Sometimes we would disagree, and Tom would call it arguing. But it was never an argument in the traditional sense. You couldn't argue with Tom, because he never properly listened in the first place. He was always in his own world, the safe world that he had created to survive his horrific upbringing. Now, in the face of our daughter's struggles, he hid, because he was terrified of failing her.

Secretly, perhaps, he wished that he could fix her with a power tool. Preferably not one made in China, though, because they're shit quality, he used to say. But there was no quick fix for her illness. We couldn't cut it out like a cancer. And so, he thought that the best thing to do would be to let me deal with Fiona. He wouldn't stand in the way. No, he would as usual go with the flow.

But what flow? Living with an eating disorder in the house wasn't a holiday. He couldn't just tag along. I craved for him to take an active part, to parent, to read at least one single thing on bulimia, an article, a blog, anything, so that he could add to the conversation instead of mumbling that I was doing a good job.

Instinctively I began to talk to myself. I discussed strategies with myself. I talked over meal plans with myself. I constantly reviewed Fiona's progress, and I carefully weighed up what to say to her, when, and how. Gradually, my monologues gained in length. When I felt like drowning in my ocean of thoughts, I would email Sally and seek clarification. Without failing, she would answer on the same day. Her messages were kind, clinical, and pragmatic. She never asked about how I managed. And I was too ashamed to cross that line.

When Alert Level Three lifted, people talked about a "new normal," they met again for coffee and wine, and Fiona made an effort to attend school in the mornings. Since her diagnosis, my world had shrunk to the size of our house, and it had left me with very little motivation to change out of the boring jeans and the old T-shirt with the paint stain on the sleeve that I had been wearing for weeks. But when my closest friend Olivia called for a second time and asked to meet for a catch-up, I decided to abandon the natural look which I had embraced in self-pity. I dug out my red nail varnish, my mascara, and lip gloss. I flicked through the dresses in my wardrobe. I held up a black one but hung it back up. *That will be the dress I wear to a romantic dinner date with Tom, one day, when life gets better,* I told myself. Instead, I chose a white dress with dark green palm leaves and beige ankle-strap sandals.

I arrived early at the cafe, ordered a large flat white, and sat down at a table near the window. I had been hesitant about disclosing Fiona's eating disorder to friends. Out of respect for Fiona, for sure, but also because in everyone's eyes, she was the perfect child who charmed people with her intelligence and outstanding manners. And I had been that proud parent who had bragged about her accomplishments and personality traits.

"I'll never have to worry about her," I had said.

Without a doubt, my friends would react with surprise to the terrible news, which would hurt like multiple bee stings. I was not sure if I had the strength for this.

I checked my phone while I waited for Olivia to show up. No message from Fiona. It was her second day in school this week without problems. I sighed and smiled to myself.

Two arms suddenly hugged me from behind as I clicked my phone shut. A whiff of luxurious bourbon vanilla travelled up my nose.

"So good to see you." It was Olivia's voice. She spun around, took a seat opposite me, let her handbag drop to the floor and smiled. She looked impeccable as always in her quality jeans and designer sneakers.

"It's been ages, really," I said delighted to see her. "You're looking good."

"So are you. How have you been?" she asked.

"All right. Yeah. Good."

CHAPTER 4

"Let me quickly get a coffee. Have you ordered already?"

"Yes, I have."

I watched Olivia walk up to the waitress. She never aged. Even though she was two years older than me, I yet had to detect a single grey hair on her. And she always talked with a soft voice. Life seemed a breeze for people like her. Single-handedly, she had raised three girls. All of them looked stunning, had wonderful jobs and husbands, lived in beautiful homes, and most importantly adored her.

When Eric was born, I had already been thirty. Olivia had had her children in her early twenties. I knew she was looking forward to her first grandchild due in a few weeks.

My phone vibrated. Fiona. Damn it! My hands shook when I texted her back: *Can't come to get you. Walk to Cafe Lucid. Olivia and I are sitting inside.*

My flat white arrived at the same time as Olivia sat back down at the table.

"Fiona's going to join us," I said. "She's finishing early today."

Olivia gave me a questioning look. I lowered my eyes, picked up the complimentary cookie and dunked it in the coffee.

"Their cheesecake looks great," she said pointing to an elderly couple who sat not far from us. "I think I'm having a piece. Can I get you one as well?"

"Sure," I said.

"Do you think Fiona would like one?"

"Oh, no, I don't think so."

Olivia waved to the waitress and half said, half mouthed, "two cheesecakes, please."

"Excited about the baby?" I asked.

"Ecstatic! I'm ecstatic!"

"Does Hannah know if it's going to be a boy or a girl?"

"No, she and her hubby don't want to know."

"I didn't know, either. Makes it more exciting."

"Mm-hmm. I've already planned to take a few weeks off so that I can help out. Just this morning, I've looked at flights to Wellington. They're quite pricey at the moment, but what can you do?"

"You wouldn't want to drive, would you?" I asked her.

"Oh, look, there's Fiona. My gosh, turning into a young lady, isn't she?"

Fiona's skin looked pale, and her eyes were glassy as she approached our table.

"Lovely to see you." Olivia stood up to hug her.

"Hi, Olivia," she said, her arms dangling like rubber down her sides.

"You look like you're not feeling well. Are you okay?"

"I've got an upset tummy," Fiona said and sat down at the table.

This gruesome school uniform makes her look even sicker than she is, I thought.

"Do you want me to order you a peppermint tea?" I asked.

"No. All good."

I saw Olivia studying her across the table. Nervously, I shifted in my chair. I knew Fiona wanted to go home. All of a sudden, I felt angry at her for putting me into this awkward situation.

"We've just got here," I said to her, hoping she would understand that I couldn't just leave right this very moment.

She gave me a flickering smile, which I took to mean that she allowed me to stay at least until we had finished the cheesecake. My thankfulness didn't take away from the tension. While my friend chatted about baby clothes and strollers, I watched Fiona. She listened and answered Olivia when asked a question, but at the same time, she checked and re-checked her phone, while texting in between with enormous speed and jittery fingers. I glanced at her bitten nails and decided that I needed to reveal the eating disorder to my friends.

The first thing Claire said to me, when I met her for brunch and filled her in, was, "Bless her. She'll have this for life."

Then she placed her hand on my arm to comfort me, her teary eyes fixed on mine while she kept repeating herself. I heard myself raise my voice as I retrieved contradictory evidence from memory, but it fell on deaf ears.

"Teenage years are difficult," my friend Zara said. "We've had our troubles, too. Last December, I found our Becky curdled up in the corner of her room crying, saying that her life had no purpose and that she wanted to walk into the nearby forest and die. The only reason she didn't kill herself was because she didn't want to abandon her guinea pigs. Thank God, we have these guinea pigs, Selina! Believe me, I was a nervous wreck for days."

My German friend, Alexa, thought Fiona should join a fitness class and work out at the gym every day. It would help boost her mood and get her hunger cues sorted.

"She's lucky to have you," she said and gave me a well-meaning hug. "I'm sure she'll be better soon. Must be hard to come up with new meal and snack ideas all the time. You don't want to feed her too much of that fast-food crap. Let me see, I'll send you some links to delicious keto recipes."

After I finally had the opportunity to tell her about Fiona's condition, Olivia never said much. She just listened. Maybe she disapproved of my over-the-top parenting style. I would never know.

Unfortunately, the more I unravelled this complex illness and its challenging treatment, the more it felt like I was talking about a far-flung country my friends had no intention of ever visiting. My plight was impossible for them to imagine, because the eating-disorder voice that I was talking about defied all logic. It was weird and invisible, and I had no photos to prove it even existed.

In the end, their concentration faded, and bulimia got confused with anorexia. As time went by, I stopped reiterating the windy explanations that I had prepared in self-defence. I would simply say that Fiona was doing better; she was almost over it, and leave it at that.

On the first weekend in April, Tom and I were invited to a BBQ at Frank and Maya's home, and I really wanted to go.

"Fiona could sleep at Anthony's," I suggested. "He'll look after her. What do you think, Tom?"

"Yes, I'm up for it," he said. "How did you know Frank and Maya again?"

I reminded him that Frank and I were both German, as if that answered the question, but to be truthful, I had forgotten where exactly we had met. Frank was a short guy with a short haircut. He was laidback and funny.

"I don't know his wife that well. I think she's from Sydney," I said. "Their daughter is in Fiona's year group."

"It'll be nice to get to know them better and meet some new people," Tom said.

I agreed.

The evening of the party, we had perfect late summer weather. It was still warm outside until nine or ten but without mosquitoes.

Frank was standing in front of his garage yelling at his bull terrier when we arrived.

"This fucking dog always gets me into trouble with the neighbours," he said with a grin on his face and then he shook our hands. "Welcome! Come on in."

He led the way through the open front door and the hallway straight onto the deck at the back of the house. Maya stood at the barbecue, poking at the meat with stainless steel tongs while smoking. She wore white jeans with a belt and a tight green T-shirt that showed her protruding menopause belly. Her blonde hair was claw clipped. As soon as she saw us, she stomped out her cigarette, lowered the barbecue lid, and galloped across the deck to greet us. She gave Tom a hug. Then she turned to me and kissed me on the cheeks.

"About time," she said.

"Thank you for inviting us," I said. "So lovely to be out of the house."

"We're glad you guys have decided to come," Frank said. "Nobody else has. They've all cancelled. Afraid to catch COVID, I reckon."

We laughed.

"Can I offer you guys a drink?" Maya asked.

"A glass of white wine would be great," I told her. Tom said that he was driving and that he would drink the non-alcoholic beer that he had brought.

"I've some sparkling," Maya shrieked, then she picked up her already-poured glass off the outdoor table and lifted it above her head in case we didn't know what sparkling was.

"Actually, I'd love one," I said.

I followed Maya into the large rustic kitchen. She poured me a glass. The island top in the centre of the room was covered with platters with different cheeses and bowls of salad. *I would prefer a kitchen island to the dining table we have*, I thought while I helped Maya bring the dishes outside. Tom went to the car to get the tiramisu that I had made and the cooler with his beers. Frank checked on the meat.

"Almost done. Tonight, we have a selection of chicken, steak, and lamb."

"Wow, that's impressive," I said.

Maya sat down at the large table and raised her glass again.

"Let's toast to the sunset," she said.

Our glasses clinked against Tom's beer bottle. We smiled at each other.

"Thanks again for inviting us," he said.

Two hours later, I was on my fourth glass of sparkling wine with no intention of slowing down, when Tom and Frank started talking about the housing market. Maya, completely bored with the topic, turned to me and lit another cigarette.

"He hates it when I smoke," she said and laughed loudly. Then she stood up to flick the ash over the guardrails. "So, how has lockdown been for you?"

I was unsure if it was Maya's happy-go-lucky demeanour or the novelty of being out of my house combined with the alcohol that made me confide in a woman I hardly knew, but I launched into an elaborate spiel about my daughter's bulimia and the difficulties of dealing with it all on top of COVID restrictions. I had been talking for about five or ten minutes when she interrupted me.

"You know it's a control thing, don't you?" she said in a sharp voice and looked directly at me.

"What do you mean?"

"You are too controlling."

"That's an old-fashioned view, Maya," I stood up and clutched my glass. "These days ..."

"No," she cut me off again and moved her face so close to mine, our noses nearly touched. "I've read a lot about eating disorders. I know what bulimia is. You need to relax your rules."

I took a few steps back. I wished I hadn't said anything. Actually, I wished I could have put my hands over my ears. *What the fuck does she know about how I parent my children?*

"We have an excellent therapist. Things are improving," I said to end the conversation.

"They say eating disorders develop when parents are too controlling during the teenage years," she repeated, slurring her words now. "Give her freedom. You're too strict."

Annoyed, I turned to get back to the table, but she came closer and trapped me between the guardrail and her body.

"I feel so sorry for you," she said, her voice still too loud for me to believe her. "Fiona is such a sweet girl. Although my daughter says she does a lot of those *nangs*."

"Huh?"

"Don't say anything to her."

"What do you mean?"

"My daughter and your daughter, they go to the same parties. You know that, don't you? I mean, she's dating Tony, isn't she?"

"Yes."

"I've been told that she and Tony do heaps of these *nangs*. You should talk to her about that."

"I don't believe that's true."

I knew that many of her friends released nitrous oxide out of little eight-gram canisters into a balloon and inhaled it for a short-lived high. Fiona and I had talked about the drug. What else was I supposed to do?

"Well, check her pockets for balloons," she said in a patronising tone.

"How's Anna doing, anyways?" I asked in an attempt to change the subject.

"She dropped out of school last week. She's living with her new boyfriend now. He's twenty-six. A hard worker. A good guy. I like him," she said. "He doesn't," she added and pointed with her glass at Frank.

"Great," I said in a flat tone and asked where the bathroom was. I couldn't care less who liked who, and if the guy who slept with her daughter was a hard worker or not; all I wanted was to curl up in my bed. When I came back from the toilet, I sat down next to Tom and told him quietly that I wasn't feeling well.

"Can we leave in ten minutes?" I asked.

He didn't mind.

CHAPTER 4

Back home, I straightaway crawled into bed and pulled the duvet over my head to shut out Maya's contemptuous voice. I decided that I wouldn't check Fiona's pockets for balloons. Then I closed my eyes and wished to airbrush the entire evening out of my life. There had been foolishness in my strive for empathy.

Bulimia wasn't a party topic.

Chapter 5

I wanted Fiona to think that her mother was solid as a rock, not weak like a crybaby. As if my peripheral toughness could brush away those doubts arising in her, now that she was eating regularly, her eating disorder was persuading her that she looked fatter than ever. I shrugged off her concerns with inexhaustible cheerfulness, and I acknowledged her courage. But it was difficult. Often she returned from school defeated, believing that her friends had noticed her imagined weight gain. A crushing day like that would always be followed by a day when she would find it too strenuous to get out of bed.

I relied on Anthony to get a break, and I knew that I owed it to him that I didn't go crazy. Despite Sally saying that a seventeen-year-old should not be put in charge of feeding Fiona, I allowed it to happen. I knew Anthony much better than Sally, of course. When Fiona had started dating him, I had taken them on a few hiking trips. I could see how he was around Fiona. Always positive and encouraging, still skipping ahead at the end of a twenty-five-kilometre day.

So, when I asked him to look after Fiona in school, I wasn't disappointed. Anthony had the perseverance and determination of the athlete that he was. Without failure, he would find Fiona during his morning teas and during lunchtimes. He would sit with her on the quad and make her eat her school sandwiches. I trusted him. Partly because Anthony was so mature for his age, but also because the alternative would have been to send Fiona to her dean during breaks, and that would have singled her out from her friends.

Anthony had instructed his mother to prepare chicken, potato, and vegetable dinners on nights when Fiona stayed over, and I gave him pocket money

CHAPTER 5

for snacks. I was glad that his mother understood that Fiona wasn't allowed to skip dinner.

When Fiona was in Anthony's care, I searched the Internet for jobs I never applied to, I leafed through magazines without reading them, and I drank far too many cups of coffee. Sometimes I would go upstairs, sit cross-legged on the carpet with my phone in my lap in case Fiona texted ... and cry.

Then, at the beginning of June, things changed. The therapist gave Fiona permission to take care of her own breakfast, albeit under my supervision. It was a huge step forward. She advised her to vary what she ate. I could tell that Fiona was doing her best to follow the instructions; nevertheless, whenever she was tense, a bowl of oats remained her go-to breakfast. It filled her up. It felt safe.

About a week into the new routine, there was a day when I agreed that Fiona could stay home, get some rest, and catch up on her photography project, because she had hardly slept the night before. It was seven in the morning, and we were already in the kitchen preparing our breakfasts. Calmly I watched how she used a measuring cup to scoop rolled oats into her bowl. Then she stirred in the almond milk and warmed everything up in the microwave. Finally, she mixed in a touch of spicy warm cinnamon while I chucked a few tablespoons of granola on my yoghurt and cut up a banana.

"Would you like a few slices?" I asked.

"No, I'm good, Mum."

I took my breakfast bowl and coffee, sat down at the table, and wrapped my hands around the hot mug. Fiona joined me with her bowl. With a degree of satisfaction, I noted that her portion size looked acceptable. *Flexibility comes with time,* I thought. Then I began a conversation, because eating in silence was hard work for her.

"Sally said you could do a sport, once or twice a week. Doesn't the school have a volleyball team you could join?"

"Nah, they're all beginners. It's boring."

"You'd probably like to pick up ballet again, I know, but it might be too triggering. What do you think?"

"I could talk with Sally about it. I mean, I love to dance. That's when I'm the happiest."

"Mm-hmm. How about tennis?"

"I'd be interested. Is there a club in town?"

"I think there is. Let me find out. We could also go to yoga together one evening a week. Yoga isn't competitive. It focuses on body strength and flexibility. That might be good for you."

"Maybe. I could give it a try." Fiona got up to put her dish in the sink. Then she turned around and said, "We need to change my bedding. I was really hot last night."

"No worries," I said and stood up.

Her night sweats were frequent now, a sign of her body not knowing how to handle the excess energy from eating more calories.

I walked into the hallway to take a fresh set of soft, white sheets and a duvet cover out of the wall closet. Before changing the bedding, I opened her curtains and window to allow some cool air to cut through the stuffy room. As soon as the bed was made, Fiona hopped on it and stuck her legs under the covers. She leaned her upper body against the headboard and returned to her social media feeds. I sat next to her and observed her silently. I hated social media, to be honest, and I was constantly arguing with myself about how to put restrictions into place that would limit her screen time. I knew it had taken over her life in a negative way. On the flip side, the virtual world seemed to distract her from the difficulties of the real world and from boredom. Instead of pondering whether the breakfast oats had been a good choice, or whether she should have had the banana slices and how many calories that would have been, a series of funny cat videos smothered these painfully ruminating thoughts. Temporarily, the eating disorder became bearable.

I saw her scrolling through her Instagram, oddly fascinated by the endless flow of interchangeable photos that her friends had posted. I glanced at the half-naked girls and tried to recall the last time I had done a cartwheel in a bikini and posted it online. (Ha!) In between Fiona's friends' posts, other photos emerged, posted by teenagers and influencers whom she didn't know personally but regarded as worth following.

CHAPTER 5

"Why are you looking at them, the influencers, I mean? They influence the way you think."

"You say the most obvious stuff sometimes," she responded.

Okay, she got it. So why didn't she care? Unimpressed by my remark, she tilted her phone to the side and moved closer to me so that I could have a better view of the screen.

"Awww, look, Mummy! Hasn't she the cutest dog ever?"

I shuddered when I saw a miniature dachshund stuck in a cotton-candy dog hoodie, sitting on the lap of a small-waisted white girl. But I wasn't surprised. I had seen it all before. Fiona had introduced me to the influencers' universe a while back. All of them had predictable and self-absorbed lifestyles, I found. While they were awake, they floated in and out of gyms in order to get a thigh gap. They sucked on green smoothies and ate healthy lunch salads with bird seeds sprinkled on top. They dressed in super cute off-the-shoulder tops and crochet shorts displaying their flat stomachs. They appeared authentic and trustworthy, almost ordinary, with almost attainable looks and lives—and that, in my eyes, was the problem.

As Fiona struggled through the dense thicket of those emotionally charged teenage years, social media made her trip over a never-ending amount of images posted by the super fit, the super healthy, and the super thin, with the super lips. And the comments of the boys in her school were in line with those who wrote on social media that they would never get with a girl unless she would put down the Bic Mac and eat a fucking salad.

Later that year, the publication of the Facebook Files, internal documents that were presented to the US Congress, in the *Wall Street Journal* would confirm my belief that Instagram made body issues worse for teenagers. One in three teenage girls was affected, they wrote, because adolescents learn from their close and distant peers what kind of body weight and shape is attractive, then they internalise it.

"Mum, let me show you a photo of Zoe," Fiona said all of a sudden.

"The girl in your class who's into swimming?"

"Yes, I think she's so beautiful. Look at her."

Grinning Zoe had shoulder-length hair and perfectly tanned skin. Her skeletal body was held together by a pink strapless bodysuit and a floral mini skirt. She was posing next to the family's swimming pool.

"Mm-hmm, yeah, she looks all right," I mumbled. "A bit skinny, don't you think?"

"She is NOT!" Fiona raised her voice. She pulled the phone close to her chest and turned her head sideways to throw me a stern look. "Leave me alone," she said.

I didn't leave her alone. I stayed next to her. The bulimia voice wasn't bossing me around as much anymore. It still made me feel uncomfortable, but I had become accustomed to it. Nevertheless, I shouldn't have said anything about Zoe's appearance. I knew better. I shouldn't have said anything at all.

I knew that the bulimia voice was never rational. It would exploit any opportunity to interpret good-looking as thin, or as fat if the comment was coming from me. I could never win. Therefore, I had begun to praise Fiona for the things that she did rather than compliment her looks. In my speech, I used eating-disorder friendly adjectives like mature, empathetic, trustworthy, and kind. I would say, sincerely, for example, that I enjoyed her company, or that her presence made me happy. It was the only way to speak to someone who measured her self-worth by her physical appearance. Fiona, however, continued to browse through other girls' profiles, torturing herself.

"Do you post much on social media?" I asked.

"No," she said. "I don't take selfies. I hate myself in photos."

"When I was young, nobody took selfies, of course. I don't even have any photos of my friends at parties. I guess we were too busy dancing, getting drunk, and kissing boys," I chuckled.

"You have said so," she said, her voice flat.

"It's egocentric, this selfie taking. Actually, I'm glad you're not posting anything. Your friends don't need photos of you. They know what you look like."

"True." She nodded.

Suddenly I remembered that my mother's birthday was coming up. "Poppy, I feel a bit like a hypocrite asking, but I was wondering if I could take a photo of you and Eric together. You know Oma can't Skype us. A photo is the only way she can see you guys grow up. She also said that she doesn't want any other presents because she's too old for accumulating stuff, and she'd throw them in the bin."

"No. I look disgusting."

"Please. Otherwise, she'll be disappointed. Nobody else will see the photo."

"I said no."

"What do you want me to tell her, then?"

"I don't know. You make it up."

I took a deep breath. I still hadn't mentioned anything to my mother about Fiona's eating disorder. Bulimia was difficult to explain to a woman who buttered her bread in a ceremonial way. After having experienced food shortages in the aftermath of WWII, she worshipped bread and butter, and she ate all her leftovers no matter how bad they looked.

Perhaps I could send her a photo of Fiona in Vanuatu, I thought. Although barely half a year had passed, Vanuatu felt quite long ago. I pulled my knees up, put both arms around them and looked out of the window.

I had the suspicion that it was Fiona's mental hunger that urged her to scroll through Instagram and TikTok. I could see that both apps fed her the food she had been denying herself for months. Their algorithms cooked up delicious meals, and her deprived eyes tasted the cheeseburgers with fries, the pasta Alfredo, and the buttery croissants. Images of calorie-rich foods brought mental satisfaction until the bulimia voice reined in the shameful thoughts and asked her to seek out low-calorie dishes, beautifully decorated health foods of colours matching the furniture in the background. When Fiona felt exhausted from the back and forth, she closed the apps. But Snapchat notifications kept reminding her about how much fun everybody else was having.

"Do you think you would benefit from deleting the social media apps or turning off the notifications, just so that you could have a break from it all?" I asked.

"No!" She chucked her phone on the ground and crawled deeper under the duvet. Slowly she turned to the side and looked at me. She had dark circles under her eyes. Her flawless skin looked pale.

"Why not?" I asked. "I'm worried about you. Comparing is not healthy. All it does is hurt you."

"I need Instagram and Snapchat, so I know what's going on. Or do you want me to have no friends?"

"But you see them in school."

"Yeah, and then I won't be able to join in the conversation because they talk about what's been posted."

"What do you mean? Surely that can't be all they talk about."

"Arghhh! You never understand anything. You're so old-fashioned. It's not the same anymore as when you grew up. We're a different generation."

"You could delete TikTok."

"I love TikTok. It's funny, and there are girls on TikTok who have recovered from eating disorders, and listening to them actually helps."

Nobody would ever be able to convince me that watching the underweight eat was helpful. But the #ED/recovery teenagers promised Fiona something that I didn't. They showed her how recovery was possible without gaining weight. Their flat bellies and protruding collarbones looked reassuring on the tough road of giving in to hunger. They told her that she could chew on zero-calorie ice chips when her hunger became too overwhelming. They told her that sleeping all day made fasting easier. And that a relapse was like spilling milk; it wasn't a big deal.

Teenagers with anorexia claimed that they had reached their set point weight and posted videos of themselves indulging in strawberry smoothies with whipped cream. They ate guilt-free, but after the cameras switched off, they rid themselves of the excess calories. It was a nasty business. But Fiona did not want to accept that. The girls that inhabited her screen had become her friends. She could rely on them. They understood what she was going through.

Although Sally had mentioned to Fiona that many of the recovered girls on TikTok were fake, she didn't ask Fiona to quit social media altogether. Instead, she recommended watching body-positive influencers who celebrated self-love. To me, it didn't make any sense. Those influencers had bodies Fiona didn't want to have. They scared her, because she didn't want to end up looking flabby and plump. But I wasn't in shape to combat social media and bulimia at the same time; therefore it drove me up the wall that Sally didn't tell Fiona to simply stay away from it all.

Fiona's fixation with watching #ThatGirl or #ED/recovery videos offered relief from feeling isolated and alone in her struggle, given that her real-life friends were less empathetic.

"Stop being so attention seeking," Eva had said.

"If you want to be Head Girl, you'd better show up in school more often," her friend Leila had added.

They felt sorry only for the girl with anorexia in their year group, because she looked like she was about to die. Fiona's bulimia wasn't visible. In their eyes, she had the perfect body. A body they envied, and yet she made a fuss about eating a fricking sandwich. *What can be so hard about that? Just bite, chew, and swallow, for God's sake,* they thought.

Secretly, I wished she had never said anything to her friends about the eating disorder, but Sally had encouraged it, and Fiona craved for her friends to be extra nice to her because she was going through so much pain. Unfortunately, she ended up becoming the victim of her own courage. Technically that was not supposed to happen, but it did, just like so much else.

As the weeks went on, the content of the therapy sessions gradually moved away from Fiona's plate and shone light onto other pathological features that hovered in the dark and were keeping her bulimia alive, such as body-image disturbance and the avoidance of fear foods.

With body-image disturbance, the emotional centre of the brain hijacks what the eyes see. It causes a constant mental note-taking of body shape, appearance, and size, which consumed Fiona all day and late into the night.

When Sally explained to me that Fiona poked, prodded, and pinched her body daily, I was stunned. Her words seeped through my body like rising groundwater through a floor. The unstoppable sadness that I felt was mixed with an almost angry disbelief. Who or what was compelling her to stare at her reflection in every window she passed? I knew it was impossible to know.

"What can I do to help Fiona?" I asked Sally during one of her sessions.

"Well, how many mirrors do you have in your house?" she asked and looked at me.

"Just one large mirror that covers the wall behind the bathroom sink," I said.

"Could you cover it up?"

"Of course," I said.

"Yes, that would help, Mum," Fiona added. She had lowered her eyes. Tears were pooling up in them. Her checks were red. I felt for her.

When our session was up, I slowly closed the laptop and placed it on the ground. Fiona told me that for months she had been wrapping her hands around her thighs and arms to measure them. She also had been assessing the size of her wrists by seeing how many fingers fitted around them. When I asked her why she felt the need to check her body every twenty or thirty minutes, she could not tell me. *Maybe she hates herself so much that she wishes her body would shrink into nothingness. Or maybe she hopes for a noticeable weight loss, but each time she is disappointed. It must be hell,* I thought.

Body checking maintains bulimia, Sally had said. But to rewire compulsive brain activity was hard work. I carefully hugged Fiona, sensing her emotional and physical delicacy, and we sat silently still for a very long time. Her fragile body was shaking under my touch.

"You're an amazing girl," I whispered. "I love you so much."

"It's so tough to stop," she whispered back.

"Just do what Sally says. Try, Poppy. She gave you some good ideas about how to distract yourself."

"Yes, she said I should delay the body checking."

"Okay."

"I'll try. Honestly."

"It takes time. Be patient with yourself, darling."

"I know."

"You're doing so well," I said. "I think we have to learn not to believe in everything our mind tells us. It tricks us. Our job as humans is to analyse our thoughts."

She agreed.

CHAPTER 5

"Right, let me find something to cover this silly mirror," I said and smiled at her. Her body relaxed. She stopped picking at the skin around her nails, and for a short moment, she leaned her head against my shoulder.

"I think the whole family will benefit from it," I continued. "I might start to believe I'm eighteen again, if I can't see my wrinkles anymore."

Fiona smiled back at me, and we both got up. She called Eva, and I went to search for some sort of a poster. In my desk drawers I came across an old fold-out world map that seemed perfect for the job. I trimmed the edges, cut off parts of Alaska and Russia, and stuck it on the mirror with so many layers of tape, that it would be obvious if Fiona tried to remove them just to have a peek.

When Anthony arrived that evening in the dark, he was covered in mud and soaked to the bone. As soon as I heard his mum's car, I went to open the front door.

"Take a hot shower. I'll warm up some dinner," I said while he took his shoes off. "Don't go into Fiona's room. She's fast asleep. She's had a tiring day. Jesus, I can't believe you guys train in this weather."

"Us Kiwi boys are tough," he said, his eyes sparkling with pride. Then he disappeared into the bathroom. I heard the shower running for ages. Anthony always forgot that our house was on tank water. Tonight, I refrained from banging at the door. Finally, he emerged in clean clothes.

"Your dinner is in the microwave. It's done. Just take it out," I said and sat down.

"What's up with the map?" he asked, shaking his head, smiling.

"I put it up so that Fiona can't see herself in the mirror."

"Oh, yeah?"

"Why? Don't you like brushing your teeth while staring at Africa?" I joked.

"Might learn something," he laughed. He sat himself opposite me and dug into a pile of mashed potatoes. Water was dripping from his dark curls. "Thanks for dinner!"

I smiled at him. Growing up in a modest household had made him such a grateful person.

"I have a favour to ask you," I said looking straight at him.

"Not another one, Mamma," he said, pretending to look unnerved. He always called me Mamma when he was joking with me. "Only if you help me with my English homework."

"No worries," I said. "We can do a bit tonight, if you're not too tired. Anyway, listen, Tony, Fiona has made a list of fear foods. Fear foods are foods that she imagines will make her gain weight instantly because they are high in calories. We know, of course that this isn't the case, unless she eats an excessive amount of them. Fear foods can also be foods that she has binged on in the past. Anyway, her therapist said that she needs to be exposed to these fear foods a lot, so that they become normalised. Eventually she'll notice that they won't make her fat. And with the foods she used to binge on, well, she'll learn to eat them in a controlled way, like slowly."

"I get it."

"We'll start with one or two at a time. I think ice cream and potato chips are on the top of her list."

"She doesn't like potato chips. She says they are disgusting."

"No, she likes them. It's her bulimia voice telling her that they're disgusting."

"So, what do you want me to do?"

"I think it'll be fun for her if you could take her out to eat ice cream rather than me buying ice cream and us eating it at home."

"Sure," he said without hesitation.

"I'll give you money to take her out. Make sure she eats different flavours and doesn't go for the sorbet type stuff. Oh, Tony, she hasn't had ice cream in such a long time."

"Mm-hmm, I know. It's annoying."

"It'll change now, hopefully."

"I can take her twice a week," he offered happily.

I knew Anthony loved everything that Fiona feared. He loved burgers, candies, and soft drinks. His parents had never told him that those things were bad for him, whereas I had labelled them as junk food and had encouraged Eric and Fiona not to eat them.

CHAPTER 5

"Do you know if she still has the calorie-counting app on her phone?" I asked him.

"Not sure," he said. "She told me that she wanted to delete the app. She mentioned that Sally had asked her to."

"Good."

"But it doesn't really matter if she has the app or not, Selina. She has memorised the calories of every single thing that she eats. She's smart like that."

"Still," I said. "It's better she doesn't use the app."

We heard Fiona's voice from the hallway: "Has the tennis coach called you back?"

Anthony turned his head. Fiona had woken up and she was approaching him in one of his crumbled-up T-shirts that looked like a dress on her.

"Yes," I said. "Fiona, you'll have your first private tennis lesson on Monday."

"Awww, great," she said. "That'll be so much fun!"

Yippee, she's looking forward to something. Maybe this will help her find some joy again, I hoped.

Monday turned out to be a perfect day for tennis. There was no wind, not even a breeze, and the afternoon sun was delicate enough that we could remove our sunglasses. All the courts were empty, since the group lessons had finished for the day. While she was practising her forehand, I unwound in one of the white plastic chairs on the deck that overlooked the courts. The sound of the tennis ball hitting her racket strangely reminded me of lemon ice cream and hot summers in Italy where I had taken my first tennis lessons. I was Fiona's age and I had had a crush on Coach Angelo. How freakish that I still remembered his name. Unfortunately, my parents couldn't afford to pay for more than a handful of lessons, so I never ended up playing tennis properly— nor kissing Angelo—but seeing Fiona run and laugh today made up for all of that. She was coordinated, and her reactions were fast.

John, her tennis coach, a gentle soul in his late fifties, liked her right off the bat. For some reason, he kept calling her Liliana, and she chuckled. After the lesson, John advised us on a new racket, and I signed her up for more lessons. While I handed John my credit card, Fiona stood next to me: sweaty, smiley, and uplifted by the endorphins of exercise and flow. She was in her element and energised ... but she never went back. As with so many other things, she couldn't give me a reason.

A week later, we tried yoga. Just once. We never returned. When I enquired why, she said, "Everyone was staring at me and judging me."

I shook my head in frustration. The yoga ladies were in their sixties and seventies. They could barely see anything without their glasses.

Nothing diverted her body-hating thoughts for long.

No happy moment was truly happy.

Day in and day out, I was forced to witness her anguish, with my hands tied. I knew that before I'd go completely insane, I'd have to come up with a plan to get us out of town in order to disrupt our daily routines. So I told Tom that I wanted to take Fiona to Christchurch for a few days to do some girly stuff with her. Tom agreed.

Two days later, I was driving South on State Highway 1, shouting to Fiona because I had asked her to put earbuds in. She was listening to rap music which I found nauseating. "Before we go to the hotel, we should go up to The Tannery and check out the secondhand clothes shop we like so much."

She gestured okay and rolled up the sleeves of Anthony's sweatshirt. She basically lived in his clothes because she had sold most of her stuff on Depop again. Sally had suggested we should buy a few items that weren't baggy, so that she could get used to seeing herself in tighter clothes again.

After a short walk through the mall, we entered the small secondhand shop. It was crammed with dresses, pants, and tops organised by colour and size, squeezed together on rows of long rails. Both of us loved to fill our wardrobes with fancy designer tags that we wouldn't be able to afford at full retail price. Rummaging without knowing what we might find always felt a bit like Christmas.

I was in a good mood when I watched Fiona cross the room to explore the retro and vintage section. I combed through a bunch of brown, beige, and

CHAPTER 5

mustardy-coloured pants. It didn't take me long to find a lovely pair of flared corduroys. I thought they might fit, folded them over my arm and continued to browse. A few minutes later, I saw that Fiona had picked out three items and was making her way to the changing rooms. I checked my phone and suddenly realised that lunchtime was nearing. Fiona needed to eat. I walked over to the changing rooms to try on the pants that I had selected. Fiona had disappeared behind one of the three curtains. The other two were also occupied. Two women lined up behind me with what looked like seven or eight items on their arms. I waited. All of a sudden, Fiona shot out, walked towards me, and then passed me. I saw that the clothes which she had taken into the changing room were now piled up on a stool. Her hands were empty and her face expressionless as if her body was saving energy.

"Can we go?" she asked over her shoulder, but it was just a formality at this stage because she was already by the shop door.

"Okay," I said, frazzled. "Let me pay for these pants. I'll be quick."

A few minutes later, I rushed out of the shop to hug her, but she wouldn't let me.

"I'm hungry," she demanded in a bossy voice.

Next to the store, there was a salad bar. The food looked like something her eating disorder could manage. As we sat down with our gluten-free quinoa salads, she told me that she didn't want to go shopping anymore, but that she wanted to go straight to the hotel room. We demolished the salads, speed walked to the car, and I raced us across the city. In under an hour, we were checked into the room.

Fiona hadn't said a word since lunch. Her face was vacant. With her shoes, socks, and jeans stripped off, she hid under the king-sized duvet. I put my bags down and wrapped the blanket as tight around her body as I could. She lay motionless in the down feather cocoon that was keeping her safe. A place both nurturing and protective where nobody demanded anything from her. What had been meant to be a fun experience had flipped on her cold turkey.

I suspected it was those bright lights and the mirror in the changing room that had made her feel inadequate and gross. I perched on the edge of the bed and placed my hand on the duvet. I waited until the anxiety had left her body.

She needed sleep. Disheartened, I got up carefully and walked over to the large windows. I looked down into the courtyard of the neighbouring hotel. People with face masks marched in circles like inmates. I forgot that the outside world was still scrabbling with COVID, because I had stopped watching the news. To darken the room and to block out reality for a while, I shut the heavy drapes. Then I sat down in the chair next to my bed and stared at the floor. *Battling with the bulimia voice is too hard,* I thought. *Why can we never win?*

Two hours later, Fiona woke up and asked to go to some of the vintage stores in the area. "They import clothes from America."

I hesitated. Then I said, "How about we avoid changing rooms for a while? I often buy clothes without trying them on. You can do the same. You roughly know your size. We just take the risk. If they don't fit, then we'll sell them again, or we exchange them."

"Are you sure, Mum?"

"Yes, totally."

The first vintage shop that we went to was closed that afternoon, but the second shop had a pair of jeans and a couple of tops that she liked. The purchase was easy, and it put a smile on Fiona's face.

The next hurdle was dinner. I chose a large restaurant with a bar and comfortable couches. *We can spend some time here, rather than sit in the hotel room,* I thought. A young man who looked like a university student brought us the menu. Eating in restaurants was tricky because figuring out the exact calories of dishes without knowing all the ingredients and portion sizes was next to impossible. I saw how her eyes scanned the pizza options, but then she quickly said, "I'm having the garden salad," and passed the menu over to me.

"Really?" I said. "Well, I'm quite hungry tonight. I think I'm having a pizza."

I knew that Fiona had been waiting for me to choose pizza. If her slim mother was having some, then eating pizza must be okay, she reasoned.

"I'm changing my mind," she said. "I'll have pizza, too, the Margherita."

To be honest, I wasn't hungry at all, but by now I was used to eating whenever Fiona ate, regardless of my appetite. Adjusting what I ate to keep

CHAPTER 5

nudging her along was just something I had to do to. What made it worse that evening, though, was that the pizzas which arrived weren't the Frisbee-sized ones I had expected, but twice as large. Without showing a reaction, I tore a piece off my pizza and lowered my back into the sofa to chew and chat. Fiona did the same. Slice by slice we worked on our meals. Fiona ate at my pace. I could tell she was hungry. Over the next two hours, she devoured most of her pizza while I talked and talked, hoping to penetrate the parallel reality in which she lived most of the time and to quieten her punishing thoughts. I never knew if I succeeded.

Before we left Christchurch the following morning, we had planned to meet Sally for the first time in person. I was excited and Fiona said she was excited, too. But shortly after breakfast, she began to act strange. A familiar ghost-like look on her face appeared, which made her skin almost transparent and her face stiff. She said she wasn't feeling well and asked me to postpone the appointment.

"No, my girl, we can't do this last minute. Don't be nervous. Sally has seen hundreds of patients who suffer from eating disorders. You know she's kind, and besides she's really looking forward to meeting you. You'll be all right."

As we walked up the path to the clinic, Fiona took my hand. She held it tight just as she had done when she was three years old and I had dropped her off at preschool for the first time.

Sally's kindness and warmth were so much more alive while we sat together in her small office than on the screen. She was praising Fiona, and her encouraging demeanour made Fiona feel reassured and positive. Nevertheless, after the session, Fiona said that she was glad to return to her home routines.

On the car drive home, I tried to portray calm, but inside I felt upset because I hadn't intended to challenge Fiona with this trip. *Was this too much too soon?* I worried. *Maybe she isn't as far down the recovery path as I thought she was.*

"Mum."

"Yes, Fiona, what's up?" I asked while keeping my eyes on the road.

"I hate my legs so much. I will never love them."

"Fiona, girl, nobody expects you to love them. Nobody. There's no need to love your legs, but please don't hate them, either. Your legs make you walk, run, and dance. You have to learn to accept them and the way they look. Altering their size at the expense of your physical and mental health is self-harm."

Fiona didn't respond. She twisted the earbuds back into her ears, leaned her head against the car window and cried, noiselessly and unhurriedly, for what must have been almost an hour while my hands bit into the steering wheel. *This damn eating disorder is a slippery fish,* I thought to myself. Every day we wrestled with it. And every day it found new ways to wriggle itself out of our tight grip. This trip had been particularly hard.

Chapter 6

Eric's speech processing disorder made it difficult for him to hold lengthy conversations. His answers were always short and literal, and his mannerisms mildly autistic. He was a silent and content boy, who smiled rather than spoke. As a toddler, Fiona had adored her older brother because he was able to read books, catch a chicken with one hand, and build sophisticated Lego cities. She had thought his quirkiness was entertaining—until she started primary school. A group of eleven-year-old boys teased Eric about the things that in her eyes made him such a cool brother. She witnessed up close how Eric was getting hurt and picked on. She was only five when it happened, and it broke her heart.

"He took the pen that Grandma gave Eric for his birthday," she said.

We were standing in the kitchen, and I was drying dishes. Her arms were folded in front of her, and she looked up at me.

"Who did?" I asked.

"A boy called Cooper. He's in Eric's class."

"I think I know who you mean."

"You need to talk to the teacher!" she demanded. "Or *I* will tell her on Monday."

"We have to be careful, so we don't make things worse for Eric."

"Cooper and his friends bully him all the time."

I had been unaware that this was happening because Eric, of course, never said a word. But Fiona was not going to keep her mouth shut. She was resolute and outspoken.

"Sometimes teachers can't do much, Fiona. Let's be careful."

"My friends Blake and Liam, they have older brothers. I can get them to beat up Cooper."

She picked up a wooden mixing spoon and swung it around as if she were the one who was going to give those boys a hiding.

"No, Fiona, I don't think that's a good idea," I said and stroked her head. "I mean, I'm glad that you tell me these things, and that you watch out for your brother, but you need to stay out of it."

"Then Eric has to learn to stand up for himself," she said, stomping her feet. "You have to teach him, Mum."

That was easier said than done. Eric had a soft nature. Even the Tae Kwon Do teacher struggled with getting him to spar. Nevertheless, in Fiona's opinion, I wasn't pushing him enough.

"You're always making excuses for Eric," she used to say.

"You are different," I would explain. "You have great social skills. Eric hasn't got your intuition. We've got to be patient. Eventually, he'll learn the correct social responses. Don't you worry, Poppy."

But she *would* worry, without me knowing. She would worry that her older brother might never have friends, never have a job or a house, never drive a car, never get married, and that she might end up being responsible for him. She would also worry that people would judge him and her for the way he behaved and looked. She had understood very early in life that what disables the disabled is society. It had overwhelmed her young mind.

"That's why I like Anthony so much," she had said last year when she had started dating him. "He's kind to Eric."

I had always preached tolerance and empathy to both my children, and it was Fiona who actively practised it in social settings outside of the family. I thought of a conversation that I had had with her one afternoon when she was eight.

A neighbour had left two orphan lambs on our doorstep. For three months, we had to bottle-feed them as soon as we got home from school. Fiona seemed to be talking like a waterfall in those days.

"My teacher doesn't understand Matthew. You know, the boy in my class who doesn't like running. She's given up on him," she said with a critiquing seriousness in her voice.

"What makes you say that?" I asked. We were locking up the garage where the lambs slept, then walked downhill through the backyard to a forested area.

"Every day she gives him the same tasks. He isn't challenged," she explained.

"How do you know?" I asked.

We climbed over a stile and followed a windy path that led to the creek that ran through the middle of the seven-hectare forest. I was walking behind her and looked down on the back of her head. A perfectly straight line divided her long hair into two braided ponytails. Shiny blue hair clips above her ears held the fine hair in place on both sides. She skipped while she spoke.

"It's why he misbehaves."

Sure thing, underchallenged children misbehave. But why did she notice and not the teacher?

"Matthew is autistic, Mum."

"Is he?"

"Yes, I know that from watching the movie with you, the *Temple Grandin* movie. He's like the girl in the movie. And a little like Eric. Like so sensitive to touch, sound, and smell. And he likes routines, but the teacher just thinks he's dumb." She turned her head, searching with her eyes for my approval.

"Oh, yes?"

"The noise from the other kids is too much for him, that's why he wears earmuffs."

"Does he sit by you?"

"I moved myself beside him. I give him things to do that challenge him, and he works."

"The teacher allows you to do that?"

"Mm-hmm," she nodded.

We had reached the creek and sat down on a small wooden platform surrounded by a grassy area with fern trees. The reflection of the leaves enhanced the colour of Fiona's lively green eyes.

She picked up a stick, dipped it in the murky water and drew random circles on the mossy planks by her feet. After a day's work in the classroom, I never felt like saying much until later in the evening. Fiona would sometimes get mad at me for that, but not today.

"Matthew is smart. When he wants to mess around, he pretends that he can't do the work." She lowered her eyes and giggled. Dimples formed that gave her a naughty look. "But I catch him out. And I make sure he gets back on task."

I wasn't astonished by this quintessential Fiona observation. Her level of interpersonal intelligence was incredibly high even when compared to the sixteen-year-old teenagers that I taught.

"His birthday is coming up next Saturday," she said. "He's invited everybody. I'm getting him a gigantic battleship. He loves models."

"We'll have to order it online, Fiona. Not sure if we'll have the time."

"Awww, please! It'll make him so happy."

Fiona was right.

At the party, after the little guests had shoved their pieces of sponge cake into their mouths, Matthew began unwrapping presents. He was unimpressed with most of the gifts.

"Have it already," he said, holding up a box with a metal detector. He then pushed it against the chest of the girl who had given it to him. "You can have it back."

Her eyes widened in disbelief. She was a skinny thing with long, curly hair.

Matthew waited for her to take the box off him, but she didn't. Instead, she started to cry. Another girl who stood behind her gave her a consoling hug. She said something that I didn't hear.

Matthew placed the metal detector on the floor. He had saved Fiona's gift for last. Impatiently, he ripped into the wrapping paper that covered the oversized carton.

"A battleship!" he shouted on the top of his lungs. "Yes!"

His fist shot in the air as if declaring a much-anticipated victory.

"He talks about her all the time," someone said. The voice was coming from a petite lady next to me.

CHAPTER 6

I turned my head sideways and recognised her as the woman who had greeted me earlier when Fiona and I had entered the house. I assumed that she was Matthew's mother. She was shorter than Matthew, and her hair was dyed a yellow blonde. She seemed overdressed in her silver sequin dress. She didn't look at me, but smiled at her son when she said, "Fiona is his best friend."

I glanced over to my daughter. She looked concerned about the upset girl. Then I turned to Matthew's mother to say something, but she had already stepped forward, parted the crowd of children that surrounded her son, pulled Fiona by the arm and made her pose for a photo with Matthew and the battleship. My eyes teared up with pride. She was such a good-hearted girl.

When Fiona was in her third year of high school and already suffering from bulimia, she told me about a girl in her class who threw tantrums.

"You won't believe what happened today," she started one evening. We were in my car heading home from her then boyfriend, Marc's place where she had spent the afternoon.

"This girl, Zaina, she's crazy. This morning, she went totally psycho and punched one of the boys in my class!" She cracked up. I could hear by the sound of her laughter that there was a sparkle of mischief in her eyes.

"You shouldn't really laugh."

"It was funny as hell. She really lost her shit. Even the boys got scared."

"Who did she hit?"

"Alan."

"Why? I thought he was a nice boy."

"He is, but she gets aggressive like that when they make fun of her. She has some sort of illness. We don't know exactly what it is. Last week, we had to leave the classroom because she started to throw chairs around. But I like Zaina. I think she's funny."

"Fiona!" I shook my head and suppressed my amusement. "How often does she lose her temper?"

"Once or twice a week."

"That's quite disruptive, isn't it?"

"Yeah, that's what the teacher said. And because of the incident today, they're taking her out of class. From now on, she has to go to the special needs unit. But I still get to see her."

"How's that?"

"Mrs. Willis asked her to select one student from our class to have lunch with every Tuesday and Thursday because they want her to kinda still feel integrated. Zaina chose me. She thinks I'm cool. And she's added me as her Facebook friend."

"That's an honour," I said. "She must trust you."

"Yeah, because I treat her normal. Nobody else does. And I know what makes her go crazy. I've studied her. She doesn't like surprises. I sort of say the same things to her every morning. And she says the same things back to me. Our little routine makes her feel safe. Nobody else really cares about her. She told me that she wants to go to the ball, and she's started messaging me about ball dresses. So cute."

"Has anyone asked her out?"

"No, but that doesn't matter. I think it's great that she's going."

Fiona never ignored anyone in distress.

She used to rescue festival goers from dehydration and binge drinkers from choking on their own vomit. She told one time she had sat in a tent next to a girl who wasn't feeling well, missing out on her favourite band playing to comfort her.

Several times, at parties, she took the car keys of smashed classmates and made sure they got home safely with a sober driver from the party or a parent.

She consoled the heartbroken who had split up with their boyfriends, and she called the upset to ask if they were all right.

Time after time she used to say to me, "Mother, I always have to keep an eye on everybody."

That's the way she saw it. For her, it wasn't a matter of choice.

The morning I spent reflecting on Fiona's past was on a day in August. Tom and Eric were at work, and I had dropped Fiona off at school. After driving

CHAPTER 6

back home through torrential rain, I decided that the weather was far too damp and cold to take Winston outside. Instead, I switched on the heat pump and brewed a pot of lemongrass tea. With the teapot and my favourite mug firmly placed on one of those bamboo trays that convert into a table, I walked upstairs. Winston followed me.

I proceeded to drag a large lime-green storage box out of my wardrobe. The box was filled with photo albums and ring binders with the kids' health records, certificates, awards, and school reports. Winston curled up by my feet between the storage box and the tray. I poured my tea, rested my feet against his warm back, and set out to look at Fiona's childhood photos and to reread her reports in the hope that amongst the hard evidence, I would find the seed of her mental illness.

I took a bulky folder with plastic sleeves out of the box. Fiona's kindergarten teachers had given it to her. The sleeves were filled with photos, artwork, and stories that they had collated. I opened it. On the second page, there was a photo of Fiona cartwheeling on the lawn.

"We were all very impressed with your cartwheeling today, Fiona! Your demonstrations encouraged some of the other children and the teacher to cartwheel, too," it read underneath the photo.

"She has advanced gross motor skills," it said on another page.

On page five, there was a photo of Fiona and her friend Elisa, both wearing red T-shirts and red skirts. The photo must have been taken on one of those days when everybody was wearing red. Fiona and Elisa had completed a team-building task, and they were smiling proudly into the camera. Then there were photos of Fiona baking cookies, painting, screen printing, and creating things out of cardboard. There were samples of her first stories about getting a cat and about a visit to the library that she must have dictated to the teacher.

I remembered how keen she had been to learn new things. The minute I would pick her up, she would tell me about a new story she had heard, or a new song she had sung, or a new game she had played. And every morning while I walked her through the metal gate into the prefabricated building and hung her little bag on the hook with her name, I felt certain that she would spend the day in a safe environment, because the place was accidentally overstaffed with people who genuinely cared. Within these walls, Fiona was able to unfold her delicate wings without fearing that someone would crush them. It was a place of solidarity.

Primary school, however, had meant a shift in paradigm. The air of solidarity was thin, and a smell of competition lingered. There were fewer teachers and more and much older kids. And there were netball mums who, when picking up their girls, chatted with the teachers and principal to make sure that their daughters would get preferential treatment. Yes, there were hierarchies. Fiona had talked about them. She had used words like "fair" and "unfair." I sipped my tea and searched for Fiona's school reports.

"She is polite and considerate and works well with others," her teachers wrote. "Her work is above the national standard. Outstanding."

Teachers had never called me with concerns. On parents' evening, they would only praise her.

"She has a different perspective on things. She sees the bigger picture. She's very mature for her age. She's a quiet leader and a great role model for the class. She relates well to her peers. She would make a wonderful Head Girl."

Fiona had always been able to work independently, to stay focused and to sit still, despite her fiery nature.

"I'm faster than the girls that go to the athletics club," she had told me.

"Because you run around with the boys at lunchtime," I had responded. "I just wish you would keep your shoes on."

It was a European thing that I feared she would step on something sharp or catch a cold. But Fiona had wanted to fit in, and at the end of a school day, the soles of her feet would be black. She was such a wild child. I remembered, one day, the school receptionist had called while I was at work.

"She flicked bark into her eyes doing backflips on the monkey bars. The school nurse has tried to remove the bark, but she can't. Fiona needs to see a doctor," she said.

My eyes wandered over to Winston. He looked at me with raised eyebrows, his snout securely rested on the ground.

"You know what else, Winston? When she was eight, she wanted to find out

CHAPTER 6

if she could fly. She leaped from the top of our picnic table onto the trampoline. Well, guess what happened? She landed on her arm, and it snapped."

I pulled out a photo album and flicked through the pages.

"There was so much life in her," I said to my furry companion. "Nothing could stop her."

While I examined the photos, I felt as if I had lost a gem in the sand. A great sadness enveloped my heart.

The stereotypical bulimia patient is a perfectionist with impulsive tendencies. I never saw the perfectionist in Fiona until much later, and therefore I wondered whether it was her wild, daredevil nature that had overshadowed her perfectionism and hidden it from me.

For years, every time we returned from her dance lessons, Fiona would rip the gazillions of bobby pins that held her bun together out of her hair, open them up so that they looked like the letter V, and throw them on the ground of her tornado-hit bedroom. They buried themselves so deep into the dark carpet that I could not see but only hear them when it was too late, when the vacuum cleaner protested with a crunching noise.

Her messy bedroom contrasted with her fussy attitude when it came to styling her hair in the mornings. Although I would try my hardest to get her fine hair neatly combed back in a ponytail, or in a bun for ballet, I could never please her. She would take one look in the mirror, pull the hairbands out and demand that I would redo everything because she had spotted a single hair sticking out.

"I'm not a hairdresser, Fiona," I would say. "Don't be like that."

Often, we would go back and forth two or three times until she was pleased with her look or until we ran out of time, and I would grab the hairspray and quickly spray everything in place. Although I had been annoyed by her pedantry, I had never considered it to be a cause for alarm. I had shrugged it off as a ballet thing.

Fiona was five when she had taken up classical ballet. It had happened by chance. The neighbour girl, Charlotte, had started going, and Charlotte's mother offered to give Fiona a lift to the studio provided that she joined

Charlotte's class. I welcomed the invitation. She would learn to appreciate classical music and the French language. She would learn self-discipline, and she would have fun dressing up in colourful costumes, I thought, so we gave it a go.

Intentionally, I would arrive half an hour before the end of class to pick up the girls. I would take a seat on the eclectic chairs in the either too-cold or too-hot corridor of the uninsulated studio, place my bag on the ground, take a deep breath, exhale the hectic day, and enjoy the sound of the piano. I would always sit diagonally across from the slightly open studio door hoping that through the crack, I could watch Fiona dance and learn about the art of ballet.

Fiona danced with girls two years older than her because Charlotte was seven. From the glimpses that I caught every week, I could tell that if the girls wanted to build correct techniques and pass their strict exams, they needed incredible dedication and perseverance. Over the years, Fiona spent hours in front of mirrors correcting her posture. She became familiar with the tiniest muscles in her body. And in order to eventually do a split in midair as if she were momentarily floating, and to balance her body weight on the tips of her toes and make it look like it's nothing, and to jump and spin effortlessly, she worked ridiculously hard. She felt, however, comfortable in a milieu of rules and perfection where one little mistake meant that her body would not make the spin or that she would injure herself.

Perhaps it was then, I wondered, *through the systematic fixing of her mistakes, that she had subconsciously adopted the illusion of control over her body, and it had become an entrenched belief.* At the time I had only ever seen her smiles, and so I naively supported her desire to dance.

When Fiona was thirteen and dance lessons started later in the afternoons, she would change into her purple leotard and flesh-coloured tights at least an hour before we actually had to leave. She would appear in the living room with her hair looking immaculate and begin to warm up. She loved our parquet flooring because she could easily slide into the splits, pirouette around the dining table, or do a handstand against the living room wall just a few inches short of hitting a painting or a bookshelf with her muscular calves. Three, sometimes four times a week, we were at the studio.

CHAPTER 6

And after ballet class, there was always another class she wanted to join, from contemporary dance to American jazz, from lyrical dance to tap. In the end, she had tried them all and passed every exam with distinction.

A photo of Fiona on stage fell out of one of the ring binders. I picked it up and held it in front of me with both hands.

"Oh, how much I adored her, Winston," I said and ran with my fingers over the photo. Fiona wore red lipstick and heavy eye make-up. She was dressed up as Tiger Lily in a yellow leotard with a golden glitter skirt and yellow tights. She smiled into the audience standing on *demi point*. For a moment, it felt as if the photo had come alive and she would dance again in front of my eyes with elegance and devotion.

I saw the image of her head tilting ever so slightly. A posture that had been so unique to her. How can a mother's heart hold so much bittersweetness all at once?

One summer when Fiona must have been nine, I had enrolled her in a ballet seminar that promised to expose her to world-class instruction. The seminar was held in Auckland's city centre. High-calibre teachers who had retired from prestigious ballet companies offered an interesting program. Fiona was thrilled about the opportunity and looked forward to spending a week in the big city.

"I've booked us a lovely hotel near the studio," I said to her.

"Does the hotel have a pool?" she asked straight away.

"No, Poppy," I said. "It's a standard city hotel. Anyway, you'd be too tired to go swimming after a whole day of dancing. The main thing is that we'll be in the city and won't get stuck on the motorway in the mornings."

"No, I won't be too tired," she insisted.

Fiona was the youngest dancer attending the seminar. Unfortunately, the first day didn't end well. She was unusually subdued when I picked her up, and as soon as we got to the hotel room, she threw her ballet flats against the wall and ripped her hair bands out.

"I'm the worst," she lamented amidst sobs, her little body shaking.

"No, Poppy," I said in a soft voice. "Come here, let me give you a hug."

I sat down on the bed, and Fiona came to sit beside me.

"That's not what the teachers said when you left. They think you're very talented. You heard it. Don't compare yourself with the older girls. But look, we can go home if you don't feel comfortable. You don't have to continue. I signed you up to have fun."

She leaned her head against my shoulder without responding.

"The teachers are lovely," I continued. "I think it's worth staying because of the quality of the teaching that you'll receive. But it's up to you. If you don't want to stay, I'm not going to be angry or anything."

The next morning, she told me, "I want to stay," as soon as she woke up. From then onwards, every day she smiled more, and her sore feet meant nothing to her. And every evening after a hot bath and dinner, she would get dressed again and ask, "Can we go up and down Queen Street?"

The first time she asked, I was baffled. "What? Now?"

"Yes, I want to get an ice cream and do something."

"But Fiona, you've danced for eight hours."

"I'm not tired."

"Are you sure?"

Yes, she was. And so, we'd go out for ice creams, and we'd buy gifts for the teachers. By the end of the week, Fiona had memorised and mastered several dances. Tom and Eric came to Auckland, and all of us watched her perform. She danced just as well, if not better than the older girls, her face beaming with joy.

A month after the dance seminar, we left New Zealand to travel for the rest of the year. Tom had taken a seven-month leave from his job, and I had taken a one-year leave from teaching. Travel had always been an integral part of our lives, ever since I had met Tom in Thailand on a backpacking trip. France was one of the many countries that we visited on the trip, and I had promised Fiona to get tickets to see the Paris Opera Ballet at the Palais Garnier.

We went on a Thursday in May 2013. Fiona had chosen a strawberry-coloured sleeveless dress and a white blazer to wear. I braided her hair. It was still light outside when we took the Metro from our Airbnb to the theatre. One of the three performances of the night was *Bolero* by Maurice Ravel. I knew Fiona would enjoy the piece because it started off soft and ended really loud.

As we entered the theatre, one of the most extraordinary and glamorous buildings in Europe, we imagined the grand foyer filled with women wearing embroidered balloon-sized ball dresses, standing in small groups with their hair in high, curly pompadours chatting to each other. Then we walked up the grand staircase, caressing the cold white-and-red marble. Fiona posed for a photo under one of the pompous chandeliers. She held a glass of cola in her hand. Her eyes outsparkling her little earrings. Then we walked into the auditorium, found our seats, flipped the red velvet seat bases down, slid into the chairs … and looked up.

"Aw, it's so beautiful," Fiona exclaimed, pointing at the painting on the ceiling.

"That's Chagall," I whispered. By now, every single seat was taken, and people had stopped talking. The lights slowly dimmed.

"Mum, a real orchestra," she whispered back, excited, and her little hand squeezed mine. And then she sat motionless like a façade sculpture. Only her eyes moved as she watched the performances with the appreciation of a ballet dancer.

Two years later, we left New Zealand for a second time with the plan to spend six months in the States. Eric attended a community college course in animal care, and Fiona went to a middle school. She was ecstatic to ride on a yellow school bus and have her own locker, just like the teenagers in the TV show *Glee*. In less than one week, Fiona had made friends with five giggly and self-confident American girls.

"Kids are really accepting here," was the first thing Fiona noticed. "Even the weirdos don't get excluded." She paused and gave me a puckish look. "I got told off today for using the word 'retarded.'"

I gasped quietly. "You didn't call someone retarded, did you?" I was shocked.

"No, of course not, Mother. It was something about the homework. I said, 'that's retarded,' but I was meaning to say, 'that's stupid.' The girls freaked out and told me I can't say 'retarded' here. In New Zealand, nobody cares."

Fiona and I talked a lot about cultural peculiarities back then. As far as Fiona was concerned, American teachers had a much better sense of humour than her teachers back home. And she loved the pop quizzes at the end of each work unit and the gerbil in the back of the science classroom that the students were allowed to let out of its cage during the last five minutes of the biology lessons—until it bit Fiona in the finger.

Unfortunately, Tom and I hadn't anticipated that Fiona would make so many tight connections in such a short time. And although everybody in the family had known from the beginning that we would only spend six months in the States, leaving turned into an unforeseen drama. I blamed myself for the bad timing. Fiona was twelve, and at that age, relationships with peers take preference over everything else. I suspected that deep inside, she never forgave us for leaving.

I poured another mug of lemongrass tea and stood up. Winston was fast asleep. He had seen enough photos. I approached the window and looked outside. The rain had stopped.

"I ought to take you for a walk, Winston," I said more to myself than to him. I began to put away the photos, but the memories remained with me humming in my heart sweetly and sadly.

"She can do anything," had been my mantra. This haunted me now every day when I woke at the crack of dawn to oversee my seventeen-years-old's breakfast. And while she would stew over what to eat, I would ask myself if I had woken up in the wrong movie.

In my head, Eric had been the one who was supposed to struggle and who I was supposed to watch carefully so that I would pick up on any early signs of depression. Fiona had always been the heroic character of the family cast. The one with the smarts and the sass. What on Earth had altered the script?

I felt cheated, but I wasn't quite sure by what or who. Not that I had ever doubted that parenting wasn't trial and error. All the same, I had tried so damn hard, and, in my view, Fiona had turned out to be the most remarkable young girl I knew. Who else was going to succeed in life if not her?

CHAPTER 6

For a brief moment, I closed my eyes. It occurred to me that I had no recollection of Fiona ever being overly joyous when she had received her dance results. She had never celebrated her successes. As soon as she received her awards and certificates, she would swiftly make them disappear into my bag.

I remembered saying to her, "Fiona, don't be so unappreciative. Give them to me. You'll destroy them, stuffing them into my bag like this."

But she couldn't care less. She wanted full marks in all her exams. And she wanted school awards for something outstanding and not because the principal had had a generous day.

She also longed for the acknowledgement of her father. In all those years that she danced, Tom had shown up for no more than two of her performances.

"Can't you do a real sport?" he had asked Fiona again and again.

She didn't know how to answer his question, so instead she had waited silently for his approval. And tried harder. At the end of each term, she would drop her excellent school report in his lap.

"You'd better study business or law when you get older and make money, being that smart," he'd say without ever reading the teachers' comments.

She would gaze at her father's face, hoping he might take those words back, her delicate inner self yearning for praise, not pressure.

Unknowingly, I had made matters worse. One afternoon, when she was ten, I burst into a hysterical fit of tears while clinging to the door frame of her brother's bedroom. Eric had not responded to anything that I had said to him that week. He had only looked at me with distant eyes. I couldn't take it any longer, and I had wept and screamed as though possessed by an evil spirit. It had frightened Fiona, and at that moment, she'd made this pact with herself that she would never be a problem. She would work hard to please me. And she would be perfect, so that I would never have to be upset again. I had only found out about this last night, when I had asked her what *she* thought had caused her illness.

She also had said that she wanted to stay in a child's body. "Growing up is scary," were the words she had used.

Perhaps puberty came too early for girls. Or for my girl. It made their bodies look voluptuous and out of proportion next to the skinny boys of the same age. Fiona, who through ballet possessed an intimate knowledge of her body, noticed these changes more than other girls, and she wanted to reverse them.

I also meditated on resilience. This had fascinated me ever since I had taught an extraordinary girl who, after years of chemotherapy, had ended up with a useless body confined to a wheelchair. But despite her circumstances, her spirit had been radiant, contagious, and unbroken. And I had known of another girl who had displayed comparable grit and determination after her mother's sudden death of cancer.

Things had fallen apart in the worlds of these teenagers, and yet I had not seen them crumble. What was it inside of them that had made them stay positive and in control? And was this something that I could have given, or still give to, Fiona?

After recounting Fiona's childhood a million times over, I began to suspect that a narrative had developed over many years in Fiona's mind that was impossible to dissect, but which had motivated her to go on a restrictive diet. It was the story that she still told herself day in day out, about not being good enough. A story that blamed her when things went wrong. A story that convinced her not only that she had to be perfect but also that that was a possibility.

I should have taught her self-compassion, I thought with regret. *I should have taught her to be her own best friend. I should have taught her that looking after oneself doesn't mean trying to fit in.*

But I hadn't, because I never thought that a girl who was so kind to others could be so ruthless to herself.

Chapter 7

The best place in town to get outrageously good, handmade ice cream was a spacious cafe with high ceilings. The walls were painted a soft cream colour and decorated with tropical plants on wooden shelves. People sat on curved benches or metal chairs. The design reminded me of the boho Pinterest images that Fiona liked. I had taken a seat at an oval table in the far corner. A waitress brought a large mocha. *I really shouldn't be consuming caffeine at this hour*, I thought. *Oh, to hell with it. I don't sleep as well anymore as I used to anyway, coffee or not.*

I took a careful sip and looked around. Most tables were empty. The place had been popular with tourists when New Zealand still had open borders. Now everybody in the industry struggled. I pulled my phone out to check my emails. Nothing new. I was tempted to tap on the Facebook app but didn't. I couldn't bear looking at the wholesome family photos that my friends posted. The last time that I had uploaded a photo must have been five months ago. A photo of Winston when we first got him.

I clicked my phone shut and looked up. That's when I spotted Fiona using her elbow to open the glass entrance door. She was typing on her phone whilst walking. *She never smiles much anymore,* I thought, giving her a quick wave.

"How was the driving lesson?" I asked her as she approached the table. "You think you're ready for Monday?"

Fiona pulled a chair out and sat down. "Can I get myself an ice cream?" she asked.

I was certain that she must have heard my question. Often, when we talked, it felt as if she would go deaf after a minute or two. Sometimes, she would turn her upper body away from me, remain still for a while, and then turn back to look at me with the face of someone who had just woken up from a serious dream.

"Sure," I answered and pulled my credit card out of the purse. "How was your lesson?"

"Mm-hmm, okay," she said, snapping the card out of my hand and getting up to walk to the counter.

I had wanted both my children to know how to drive a manual car. Eric had passed his test a few years ago under the gentle instruction of a small, square-looking man with a strong Irish accent. Fiona, on the other hand, had convinced the instructor to switch to automatic after the first two lessons.

"You haven't really given it a fair shot," I had said.

"You're not me, so you don't know," she had answered.

Most of the time when I had picked her up after a lesson, she wouldn't talk to me for at least half an hour. I would keep quiet myself. I imagined that it must be draining to learn all these new things that weren't muscle memory yet when your brain was on permanent fight-or-flight mode. And I feared that she would beat herself up for making mistakes. The only reason why Fiona hadn't given up altogether was because she wanted her independence.

Poor girl. I watched her check out the large variety of ice cream flavours. She looked as if the fifty-minute lesson had zapped the life out of her. Without ordering anything, she turned around and sat back down.

"I'm waiting for Anthony," she said. "He's coming in five."

"I figured as much," I said with a grin. "I bet he wants me to pay for his ice cream."

"Yes," she said in a bland voice.

Anthony and she had been coming to this cafe for the last few weeks to practice eating gelato.

"So, are you confident about your driving test on Monday?"

"No. But I don't want to talk about it right now."

"Okay."

We said nothing for several moments. Suddenly, I noticed how her left leg shook uncontrollably.

CHAPTER 7

It must have been last week when I had seen it for the first time. We had been sitting at the kitchen table. The leg had moved so violently that I had wondered if subconsciously she had wanted it to fall off, just to get rid of it, or whether there was another person inside her that shook it.

"Is there something wrong with your leg, Poppy?" I asked now.

"What?" She looked perplexed, as if I had spoken in Portuguese. Her phone dinged to notify her of an incoming text. She immediately turned her head toward the door. Anthony came bolting into the cafe, a powerful energy radiating from his body. He was wearing a white T-shirt and sport shorts. As usual, his uninhibited presence stood in sharp contrast to Fiona's rigid self-consciousness. With my card still in her hand, she got up and asked Anthony what he wanted. He was quick to decide, then he leaned forward to give me half a hug and sat down.

"What's up?" he asked cheerfully.

"Not much," I said.

"How's the stock market? Made your millions yet?"

"I wish," I said and shook my head. I had taught myself how to trade with the small amount that we had in our savings account, since banks had stopped paying interest rates.

"Come on! You're just not telling us."

"It's a learning curve, this trading, that's for sure. But, hey, markets aren't bad right now."

"I should give you some money to invest."

"Well, only if you can spare a little more than just fifty dollars, Tony." I grinned at him.

"I better stop spending so much money on takeaways then and start saving," he said.

"Good idea," I agreed, and we both laughed.

Fiona returned with two equal-sized ice cream cups.

"You need to go to the counter and show them your vaccine pass," Fiona said to Anthony and sat down.

"This girl, Melanie," she was talking to me now, "remember, Mum? The one who used to go on those long runs with her mother. I've told you about her."

I nodded.

"She's come back from Christchurch. She says that she's recovered. But I don't believe her. I think she's still not eating enough."

"Mm-hmm." I never really knew what to say when she made comments like that. Why was she trying to be other people's therapist? I glanced over to Anthony who stood at the counter and wondered if he cared as much about Melanie's eating habits as Fiona did.

"I've decided to spend time with her during lunch breaks because she hasn't got that many friends," Fiona said poking with a wooden spoon at her vanilla ice cream.

Oh, no, I thought. *This can be far too triggering.*

"How's Eva these days?" I asked. "Aren't you hanging with her anymore?"

Fiona didn't answer my question; instead she continued to talk about Melanie. "She wants me to support her with her eating when we go to the summer festivals."

"Well, that's still months away," I uttered, relieved, picked up my cup and slurped the mocha to get a better taste of it.

"I'm staying over at his tonight," Fiona said, looking at Anthony, who was back at the table. "We'll be going to a party."

"Is your mum picking you up, Tony?" I asked.

He nodded and shoved a spoonful of sugary deliciousness into his mouth.

"So, how many beers are you planning to have tonight?" I teased Fiona.

"Why are you asking? You know I drink cruisers. Actually, I've discovered these sugar-free ones. They don't taste too bad," she said.

"Cruisers are pussy drinks," I said in a joking manner.

Fiona threw me a reproachful look while Anthony laughed. He knew I had only said that because he sometimes drank them too, and I was trying to persuade him to be a real man and avoid the premixed rubbish.

"None of the girls drink beer because it makes your belly stick out," Fiona said.

Back when I was a teenager, girls drank beer because it was cheap. Nobody worried about their belly sticking out. I knew, however, that if I begged Fiona to let go and to have a good time, even if only for one single night, it would backfire.

I looked at my watch. It was half past four. "Well, I'll leave you guys to it. I'm shooting home now." I got up and rested my hands on Fiona's shoulders. "Oh, you still have my card."

Fiona slid the card in my bag. I promised to pick her up from Anthony's early the following morning, and I left the cafe.

When I came home, I saw that Tom's company car was already parked next to my spot. I rushed into the house. My husband greeted me with a glass of red wine in his hand. Usually this meant that someone at work had pissed him off, but maybe not tonight.

"Hi, darling," I said. "Good to see you're home early. Dinner's ready. I just have to warm it up. Everything all right?"

"Couldn't stand it anymore," he said. "Would you like a glass? I'm not hungry tonight. I had a big lunch."

"Oh, well, we don't need to eat," I said, quite relieved. "I'm really not that hungry myself." I dropped my handbag on the kitchen counter and bent down to pat tail-wagging Winston. "But a glass would be great, thank you."

"Where's Fiona?" he asked.

"She's with Anthony tonight."

"How is she?"

"Let's sit together on the sofa, and I'll fill you in. We haven't talked about her in a while."

I knew Tom had been hoping for a different response. Sit-down sessions drove him crazy because he felt that I lectured him. Nevertheless, as we sat side by side on the couch, knees touching and wine glasses resting in our laps, I began.

"Actually, she's doing quite well when it comes to eating independently," I started off. "She prepares all her meals by herself now, besides dinner, and as far as I can tell, the portions that she serves herself look good. Every once in a while, she even asks me for a second snack later in the evening. Sally seems content with her progress."

"I'm happy to hear that," Tom said. He unbuttoned the top of his dress shirt with one hand and smiled at me.

"Last week she joined the gym, and with Sally's permission she's going twice a week."

"Yes, you said the other day."

"I personally think gyms are toxic, but that's what they've agreed on. Last time she went, she came back mumbling something about the fitness instructor being a recovered bulimic. 'He's so understanding, I really like him,' she said. God knows. To me, he looks like someone whose bulimia has turned into an obsession about muscle size. Gyms can be so dangerous. The mirrors, the people. I wish she wouldn't go."

I paused and rubbed my eyes.

Tom leaned back into the cushions.

"Is that why she bought this high-dollar protein powder stuff?" he asked.

"Yes, every day she puts a spoonful in her milkshake. It's full of chemicals, but dare I say anything, she'd blow up on me. Next time she wants to buy it, I'll tell her we don't have the money."

"Well, we don't."

"Look, part of what is unsettling me is that the format of the therapy sessions has changed. I only get to sit in with them during the last five minutes. That's when Sally gives me a brief summary of what they've talked about. I don't like it, although I understand why. Both of them have moved on to discussing adolescent topics. My presence would inhibit Fiona. Still, I feel excluded."

Tom shrugged his shoulders. We both sipped on our wines for some time. I noticed a few grey hairs right above his left ear. He had always looked much younger than me, even though he was two years older. Now it seemed he was catching up.

"Would you like a top up?" he asked and rose from the sofa to get the bottle.

"No, I'm good," I shook my head. "I'm worried about her mood. She's so volatile. But it's not just that. When she isn't angry, she's low. Lately, it's getting harder and harder for me to make her go to school."

"Have you told Sally?" Tom asked.

"I have. I've emailed her about it. I've told you, every week I share my concerns and observations with her. She never asks me to. I just do it. I think it's important that she also gets our perspective on things. Fiona might lie to her."

"And?"

"She wants me to take Fiona to the GP and put her on antidepressants. Not sure if she's said anything to Fiona."

"No way."

"I agree, Tom, but at the same time I'm scared. You know why. We've got to do something."

"You'll figure it out."

"What do you mean?" I raised my voice.

"She's been snappy with me for months."

"What are you talking about? Do you really believe that she's all nice when *I* talk to her? She flies off the handle all the time. By the way, she went to the hairdresser's yesterday."

"Not again? How short is her hair now?" Tom pulled a face. He hated short hair on women.

"It's chin long," I replied, staring at my half-empty glass. "Oh, well, it doesn't matter. Please say you like it when you see her tomorrow."

Tom stood up to get his phone and sat back down.

"Don't take it personally, her snappiness, I mean. I think I'll write to Sally saying that I'm going to buy supplements that will help Fiona with her mood. I'll get some St. John's wort. That's what people use in Germany for depression, and I'll also get some 5-hydroxytryp-something, vitamin B12, and Omega 3 fatty acids."

"Sounds good," Tom said and topped up his glass. "Want some more now?"

"No, thank you," I said. *I never drink much anymore these days, which is a good thing, I suppose.*

"Have you asked Sally for how much longer Fiona will have to be in therapy?"

"No, I don't dare. Well, actually, I don't think she can answer that question anyway." I sighed. "According to the book that I've read on family-based therapy, the treatment is about six to eight months long. We've been with

Sally for about six now. Somehow, I have this feeling Fiona needs quite a while longer. In any case, we definitely shouldn't stop the treatment until she's fully recovered. And by that, I mean one hundred percent."

"But she eats well, you said?"

"She does," I squinted at Tom and took a deep breath. "Regardless, there's still so much unhealthy stuff going on in her head."

"It's the phone. The stuff she watches."

"Yes, I agree. Not to mention that the eating disorder has given her all sorts of other anxieties."

"She's got those from my mother."

"No, she hasn't." I laughed. "You don't inherit anxieties."

"Do you want to watch a movie?" he asked, maybe because he wanted to avoid an argument, and he stood up.

"Not really," I said.

Tom knew that his question had been merely a rhetorical one. I hated watching mindless Hollywood crap. It was all the same to me. I would rather just sit and talk. To his credit, he never complained. He walked into the Netflix room and scrolled through the movie options. He was lucky. He could numb his sorrows with a film, whereas I could never switch them off.

I poured my wine down the drain and made tea. Then I went upstairs to sit on the carpet, lean my back into a beanbag, and think. In the past, I had called friends in the evenings, but I didn't do that anymore. I didn't want to bore them with yet another episode of "Family Life with an Eating Disorder." They, like Tom, were wondering why recovery was taking so long. And they reminded me that I had said that she hadn't been purging anymore. Last time they had seen her she had looked so well, not at all emaciated. She was such a pretty young lady. So, she was over it, wasn't she? Healed.

I pulled a large Alpaca blanket out of the basket near me. I had bought it in Ecuador a few years ago, and it kept me warm whenever I began to shiver. Although we lived in a cosy house, I shivered in the evenings. It was tiredness. I wrapped the blanket around my legs and stared at my untouched tea and my unopened laptop.

I thought about how unlucky Fiona was that we lived in times that idealised brutal thinness and extreme fitness. Our cultural environment triggered new types of eating disorders. Although people often mentioned that bulimic behaviour already had been prevalent during Roman times (after all, they had vomitoriums), I couldn't see thinness being idealised in those days. The binge eating and purging of the Roman elite had little to do with today's bulimia.

Nor had the early descriptions of *anorexia hysteria*, a term that was used in the days before it became *anorexia nervosa*, mentioned a desire to be thin. Having had religious connotations, anorexia had been associated with purity.

While bulimic behaviour had been around for some time, it had only become a thing when I was about thirteen years old. Maybe that's why I had never known much about it. In 1979, Gerald Russel, a British psychologist, described for the first time patients who seemed to suffer from a strange binge-and-purge syndrome that didn't quite fit the diagnostic criteria of anorexia. He named the syndrome bulimia. Two years later, *The New York Times* published an article about a secretive phenomenon which appeared to start with dieting and which was infiltrating college campuses in the States. Then, in 1987, bulimia became an official medical diagnosis with its inclusion in the DSM-III. After that, this rare disorder developed into a social virus, spread around the globe and was now being romanticised on social media. That's how I saw it.

I heard Tom opening the fridge.

"Could you do me a favour and check my phone, please?" I asked in a loud voice. "Maybe Fiona has texted."

"Hold on," he said. "No, she hasn't."

"Good. How's the movie?"

"All right. I'm going to bed soon."

With a flush of anger, I kicked my laptop away from me. The release felt good, but it was only masking my pain. As much as I wanted to learn more about bulimia, it was the same story every time: I would start watching a promising talk or begin reading an interesting looking article about eating disorders, when a few minutes into it, I would realise that it exclusively explored anorexia. I was sick of it. In a weird sense, I began to feel left out. Of course, I knew that eating disorders overlapped and that some of the information also applied to people suffering from bulimia. But still. Why did they do that?

I reflected on Fiona's earlier comment, the one about Melanie. She had wanted me to think that she was worried about Melanie, but I was convinced that she only pretended to be concerned because people with anorexia were the envy of other patients with eating disorders. As unbelievable as it sounds, Fiona envied Melanie. Like most people with bulimia, she judged her eating disorder through the lens of anorexia; this meant that in her eyes, people with anorexia were the ones who succeeded at being thin and bulimics were the ones who failed at being anorexic.

Not really losing weight makes you feel worthless, and *I am disappointed in myself for not having enough self-control to be anorexic. Being anorexic is better than bulimic*, I read in one of the eating disorder support forums. Someone else had posted: *No illness is better than the other because they all pretty much lead to death.*

But sadly, bulimia patients often receive less attention from medical professionals and councillors than anorexic patients. This only reinforces their belief that they are not sick enough to deserve treatment. And so, they continue to hide their self-destructive and shameful behaviour, just like Fiona had done.

I remembered an incident that was another perfect example of the secrecy and shame that surrounded bulimia. It had happened about a week ago. Fiona and I were walking through town shopping for stationery when Fiona poked her pointy elbow into my rips.

"Do you see Nancy over there?" she asked, her eyes looking across the street.

"Oh yes, I remember her," I said. "She was at your birthday get-together. Do you want to say hi?"

"She has bulimia," Fiona responded quite matter of factly.

"How do you know?"

"She posted something about wanting help, but then she quickly deleted it. I had read it, and I private messaged her and asked her what her post was about. She told me that she's been throwing up for over a year now. She's

CHAPTER 7

thinking of dropping out of school. I was wondering if you could maybe speak to her, since you know a lot of stuff about bulimia?"

"Anytime," I said. "But what about her parents?"

"Her parents don't know. She can't tell them. They'd freak out."

"But they need to know."

"I know," Fiona said, "That's why I want you to talk to her first and explain. She's so afraid. She'll never get better on her own."

"Poor Nancy," I said. "Tell her that I'm more than happy to chat with her. She can come to our place, if she wants to."

Nancy never showed up, despite us making several arrangements to meet. Every time, she would find an excuse, usually sending Fiona a last-minute text.

Sometimes I asked myself how beneficial the rigid clinical distinction between anorexia and bulimia really was for those that suffer from bulimia. Didn't it foster competition? And wasn't the reality fluid, with certain patients moving back and forth between the two disorders? Patients with anorexia who suffered from the binge eating and purging displayed the same behaviours as patients with bulimia. Weight was the only difference between the two. But I kept reminding myself that I didn't have the expertise of a psychologist and that the clinical distinctions probably made sense in the medical world.

My knees started to ache. I got up and searched for the organic sage incense sticks that never failed to bring tranquillity to my frayed nerves, when from behind I heard the staircase squeak.

Tom came to give me a kiss. "Good night, darling," he said. "Coming to bed?"

"In a minute," I mumbled, but I would wait until he was asleep, because on nights when my head was filled with sorrow, my body didn't want to be touched by desire. Perhaps it would have been different if Tom and I were more connected. So, before I walked downstairs to warm up my tea in the microwave, I softly shut the bedroom door.

Standing in the kitchen, I rested my eyes on Winston. He was stretched out in his basket where he slept when Fiona was not around. He opened his eyes to look at me. I smiled at him. I was thinking about the last conversation that

I had had with Sally. Fiona wasn't suffering from depression. She didn't have that kind of personality. Okay, sometimes she felt a bit down, but most of the time she slammed doors and shouted around the house with her voice set at the highest volume. I mean, of course, she wasn't feeling great. Who would with an eating disorder? I frowned. This co-morbidity depression talk that the therapist and Fiona had started was pissing me off.

"Why do people always have to label everything?" I asked the sleepy dog. "It serves no purpose. All it does is scare people and tick boxes. Our Fiona isn't depressed. Sally just needs to make her work harder on rewiring her brain, do cognitive stuff. But they exclude me now, you see. I'm out of the loop."

One Monday that September, Fiona refused to go to school. She felt low, she said. On the two days that followed, she still insisted that she wasn't feeling in good shape and her stomach was sore. Come Thursday, I sat on her bed and demanded an explanation for her lack of motivation.

"What's going on, Fiona?" I asked. "Come on, sit up. Let's have a chat. I can't help you if you refuse to let me know what's bothering you."

"On Sunday, everybody went to the beach," she said, tears rolling down her cheeks. "But nobody called me. Not even Eva."

"How do you know they all went to the beach?" I asked. "You haven't been to school."

"I saw it on the Snapchat map," she sobbed.

"What do you mean?"

"Mum! I can see where everyone is. Look." Fiona held her phone screen under my nose.

"You guys are spying on each other!?" I raised my voice. "I tell you what, your generation is truly driving me up the wall. The stuff you guys do is unbelievable. Don't you value your privacy? Just don't even look, Fiona, for crying out loud!"

"You're not being helpful."

I immediately regretted my irritation. "Maybe Eva thought that Julia had let you know, and Julia thought that Leila had told you. You know how that goes sometimes. It might not have been intentional," I tried.

"No, it wasn't like that."

"How do you know? Have you fallen out with them?"

"No," she said. Her words were barely audible. "They don't want me around." She paused. "They don't like me."

I panicked because it hadn't escaped me that Fiona's circle of friends had left her out a couple of times lately. Part of the problem was that she was dating the hottest guy in school. Her girlfriends were envious because they all wanted to go out with Anthony. And they didn't comprehend what the hell Anthony saw in his neurotic, attention-seeking girlfriend. He should be dating one of them, someone normal, that's what they probably thought, but I was unsure if Fiona understood this.

I took a deep breath, realising that her gradual social exclusion had the potential to undo all the hard work that we had been doing for the last six months. I folded my hands and spoke slowly and softly so that Fiona would not think that I was fearful.

"Why don't you invite Kim around, or Carl and Joe? They're nice. I mean, you could enlarge the friendship group. Include more boys. I always got on better with boys than girls when I was your age."

"Good idea," she said, and her face brightened up.

"All right, Poppy, now it's time to get up and leave your room and do something productive, and tomorrow you'll go to school."

Fiona burst into tears. "I'm too upset. I can't, Mum. Everything seems a huge effort. My arms and legs feel really heavy. You don't understand."

"Have you spoken with Sally about it?"

"Yes."

"And what does she say?"

"She thinks antidepressants would help."

I knew it. "Well, you know what I think about them. In most cases they do nothing, but get you addicted."

"I know. I just can't bear it anymore. I want to be happy again."

"How about we try supplements first? They'll take a little while before they kick in, but they might help. I've ordered four different supplements that are recommended for depressive mood. They should be arriving within the next two days. You could give it a go. What do you think?"

"Okay."

"And then, if things won't improve, we'll go to the doctor. Does that sound good?"

Fiona nodded.

But when I shared this plan with Sally, she remained skeptical. She was convinced that Fiona needed serotonin uptake medication to finally see the light at the end of the tunnel. I disagreed, believing that Fiona was suffering from recovery fatigue, an extreme physical and emotional exhaustion. Having to defend myself made me cranky, and my emails began to sound tired. At night, I would lie in bed wishing Fiona's friends would treat her with kindness, wishing Fiona's internal battle would finally end, wishing for this all to be over. But it wasn't.

Two weeks later, despite taking the supplements, Fiona was pleading with me to take her to the doctor to get antidepressants. We did.

"The medication could evoke suicidal thoughts, but they should pass within the first few weeks," Dr. Stevens explained. "I'm starting you on a very low dose."

Fiona appeared relieved. I swallowed hard and looked at the ceiling. I felt my heart racing. I was on high alert.

After the doctor's visit, Fiona displayed an unusual lightness in her movements. She chattered away while we walked down the new pedestrian zone in town, looking for a pharmacy that was open after five. As soon as we got home, she invited me into her bedroom. She asked me if I had the time to watch a short video with her. I sensed her eagerness to share something with me that had been brewing inside her.

We huddled together on her bed. Fiona covered our touching thighs with a pillow and placed her laptop on it. She searched through her reading list and clicked on the page of an online bulimia recovery coach called Isabel. Then she flicked through a long list of blog entries with a speed that indicated an intense familiarity with the site, until she found a video titled "Extreme Hunger." I put my arm around her shoulders, and she leaned her head against my chest. For a short while, her young body trusted my old body. *Perhaps we are doing the right thing, I thought, and Fiona's symptoms will disappear with the medication. Before we know it, she will be out the other end.*

I took a deep breath and directed my attention to the online coach. I was pleasantly surprised that she wasn't a girl in her twenties but a middle-aged British woman who wore ordinary clothes. Her high forehead and dominant nose reminded me of a younger version of Meryl Streep. She sounded subdued and caring, like a primary school teacher, when she said that extreme hunger was a natural part of the recovery process. The malnourished body requires an unusually high number of calories to make up for all the calories it had been deprived of during the starvation phase, when organs, muscles, tissues, nerves, and bones were severely damaged. After periods of starvation, the body needs an incredible amount of energy to repair itself, with some recovering patients having to consume more than 5,000 calories a day.

Eating that many calories is a massive challenge because the person recovering from bulimia would often agonise over having developed a binge-eating disorder. But this is not the case, she explained. Extreme hunger is not the same as binge eating. It is internal restoration. If you want to recover, you need to give in to extreme hunger. She made it sound like a sales pitch.

Without warning, Fiona paused the video even though it still had a few more minutes to go. She turned her face to look at me. I saw tears in her eyes, but she held on to them. "That's what it's like for me. I never feel full."

I didn't know what to say. The fact that I needed to serve Fiona twice what I have been giving her seemed as unfathomable to me as having missed her huge hunger.

"Wow, Fiona. I'm glad that you shared this video with me. Why have you never asked for a second helping or dessert?"

"It's scary to eat so much."

"Mm-hmm, but apparently that's what you need to be doing. There's a reason why you're so hungry, plus you're still growing."

"I'll end up huge."

"No, you won't. Don't be silly. That's the eating-disorder voice talking." I stroked her back. "So, is this why you eat the protein powder?"

She shook her head, but I knew I had nailed it. Weight-loss programs recommended the consumption of protein to suppress hunger. It must have helped Fiona to feel satisfied for longer.

"I like Isabel," I said and kissed Fiona's head.

"I do, too," she said.

I let my hand glide over her silky hair. *Did Fiona want me to watch this video because she felt that only a thin woman who had recovered from bulimia would be able to normalise her insatiable hunger?* She obviously didn't want me to think she was a greedy binge eater. I pressed my lips together. Why had I never asked her to have dessert? Or was it that I had also been guilty of trying to take shortcuts on the road to recovery?

"Do you know what I think, darling? Those salads and vegetables that you've been eating won't do the trick. Salads are too difficult to digest anyway. I think you've got to eat more calorie-rich foods, like chocolate and red meat."

"I'm not sure if I can do that," she whispered.

"It's the only way forward. You have to learn to trust your body. Initially, you might gain a little bit of weight, but your body has a set weight, and after the extreme hunger has subsided, it will go back to that set weight."

"That's so terrifying!"

"I know, but your body makes better decisions than your eating disorder when it comes to your health."

"Sometimes I feel bloated while I eat. My belly feels rock hard."

"I understand. Your digestion isn't working properly, but ironically for it to work again, you need to overeat for a while. Look, really, we can do this together."

"I don't want to talk about it anymore," she said abruptly in a voice that made me shut up.

I continued to stroke her scared body until her breathing slowed and she closed her eyes.

In order to gain control of her life, she had created a second self that inhabited her mind and body. Now she didn't know who to trust. Her life was more out of control than ever before.

CHAPTER 7

I looked down and watched my sweatshirt absorbing the tears that had begun to stream down my face. Overcoming this extreme hunger was going to be one of the greatest obstacles of the recovery process. I was afraid for her.

During the following months, Isabel and her video clips became a new line of communication between us. On nights when Fiona was plagued by extreme hunger, wrestling with food calculations, and wondering whatever else was happening to her, I would suddenly get a notification on my phone. She would send me a link to the video she was watching. In this way, without the need for long questions and complicated answers, Fiona indirectly gave me access to her thoughts.

And Isabel with her no-frills explanations converted scary and shameful behaviours into normal processes. I was happy that we had come to this tacit arrangement, because I felt that during the past months, I had been too intrusive. But being the sort of person who rips into packages instead of looking for the "peel here" label, I struggled with patience.

"The meds make me feel completely numb," Fiona complained one morning.

"I guess that's what antidepressants do," I replied and shrugged my shoulders. "They dull everything."

"I don't want to take them anymore."

"Do you think you've tried them for long enough?" I asked. "It's only been three or four weeks, hasn't it?"

"Yes, but now I don't feel *anything* anymore. I hate it."

"We need to let Dr. Stevens know, because you can't just stop taking them."

"Yeah, although I think I can, because I'm on the lowest dose."

Just to be sure, I called Dr. Stevens, and he confirmed that Fiona could stop taking her medication.

A few weeks later, Fiona asked if she could borrow my car. She had passed her driving test and, every so often, she had been taking herself to school. I was about to go for an early morning walk with Winston.

"I'll be back in ten minutes," I said. "Let's have breakfast together. But, yes, sure, you can have my car. The keys are in my coat pocket."

I was delighted to see that she was already dressed in her school uniform. I quickly snatched my coffee mug, slipped into my crocs, and called Winston. September was coming to an end. It was one of my favourite months because the kowhai trees brightened the sleepy winter garden with their yellow flowers announcing spring. I picked up a stick and threw it for Winston. First, he chased after it, then he halted in his tracks to seize a piece of flax instead. He loved to race around in large circles whilst dragging long pieces of flax behind him. I strolled up to the fence line where I had planted a row of blueberry bushes the previous year. From here I could see the morning mist on the rolling hills in the distance. I stood for a few moments to enjoy the view. Then I bent down to yank the flax out of Winston's snout and threw another stick. He took off and then he sped up to chase after a rabbit. He returned unsuccessful and panting.

"Ha, these rabbits are too fast for you, aren't they?" I laughed. "Let's go see Fiona. Go!"

When I arrived at the front door, he was waiting to be fed. I sat down on the wooden shoe box next to the entrance until he had licked his bowel clean. Before entering the house, I wiped his paws with an old towel that hung above the box. I called Fiona. No response. *She's got her earbuds in again*, I thought, and started setting the breakfast table.

"Come on, girl! Let's eat!" I yelled.

Nothing. I went to open her bedroom door without knocking. That's when I found her changed from her school uniform into sweatpants and the T-shirt she had slept in.

"What's going on?" I asked.

"I can't go to school, Mum. I can't focus. "

Although her grades were surprisingly good, my blood started to boil. I suspected that she was using her eating disorder as an excuse to stay at home, but I didn't say anything. She came to eat her breakfast oats and then she stretched out on the sofa. I pulled up a kitchen chair.

"Has anything bad happened this morning?" I inquired.

"No," she replied, but she looked miserable.

CHAPTER 7

"Why don't you go into school for your first two lessons and then see how you feel?" I suggested.

"No."

I broke out in a sweat. On average she would attend only two or three days a week, but until now I had never said anything about her missing school.

"Please, Fiona."

"I said I'm not going." Fiona hid her face behind her phone screen, signalling that I was wasting my time trying to persuade her.

"Okay, stay home, but you're doing schoolwork, and later this afternoon, you'll go for a walk with Winston. I will not have you on your phone all day. In an hour, I'll switch the modem off. You shouldn't be talking to your friends while they're sitting in class."

"You can't do that," she argued.

"Yes, I can," I said and got up.

"No, you can't," she screamed and then ran into her room and slammed the door behind her.

I walked into the kitchen and leaned my body against the fridge.

We could be so happy here. This was such a beautiful property in such a beautiful town so close by the ocean. I don't think I can do this any longer.

I took our dishes off the table and put them into the sink. Then I stood with my hands holding onto the counter while I bit my lower lip thinking that this was going to be a difficult day. I heard a sound, no louder than a timid breeze. I thought it might be Fiona's bedroom door opening. I heard steps. Vanity drawers were hastily opened and shut. To this day I have no idea why I shot through the kitchen and hallway to check what was going on in the bathroom. I had never followed Fiona into the bathroom since she was a little child.

She was standing in front of the sink when I came in. Her hands clenched into fists. She looked at me nervously. I didn't know what to say to her.

"What are you doing here, Mum?" she yelled.

"I'm not sure," I said.

"Go! Go away!" she screamed freakishly.

When I didn't move, she pushed past me, bolted into her bedroom, grabbed my car keys that were buried in the folds of the duvet and rushed to the front door.

"I'm taking your car," she shouted.

"No, you're not!" I tried to sound stern.

Now standing next to her, I watched how she hastily squeezed her feet into her untied shoes. A part of me wanted to grab her arm and pull her back inside the house and lock the door, but I knew she would have fought me off.

"Where are you going?" I asked.

"I'm going to school."

"You don't have your school uniform on."

"I don't need to," she said in a quieter tone. "I'm going to see the councillor."

Then I watched her run to the car. I entered the house. I needed to sit down before my knees gave way. Hearing my car race down the driveway at full speed frightened me. My vision became blurred.

Sometimes there's nothing we can do but be still.

After sitting paralysed for what must have been at least half an hour, my phone rang. I saw that it was Mrs. Paladino. I let it ring a few more times before picking up. I already knew what she was going to say.

"Are you at home?" she asked. "I have Fiona and Anthony with me right now. Fiona wanted to take her life this morning. You need to come and get her, please."

I was silent. Shocked. But on some level, not surprised.

"Are you with me?" I heard her ask.

"Yes."

"Could you come into my office, please?"

"Yes."

Shaking, I knocked on Eric's door and asked to borrow his car. Still shaking, I drove to school. When I arrived at the councillor's office, I regained my composure. Fiona was in floods of tears. Anthony sat across from her, speechless.

"She had about seven or eight paracetamols in her hand," Mrs. Paladino said.

I had come into the bathroom just in time to stop her.

CHAPTER 7

"Fiona told me that she is regretting it," Mrs. Paladino added.

How could she, when I love her so much?

I brushed aside the incredible hurt. Getting up and doing something felt good now. I needed to be in control again. I took Fiona home with me. She sat silently next to me on the sofa while I made several phone calls. I rang Sally, and we made an appointment for the afternoon. Then I rang Dr. Stevens. I asked to see him immediately. In conversations with the councillor, GP, and therapist, Fiona came to understand that they cared, that she was no burden to anyone, and that her mum, dad and brother loved her very much.

Tom came home early and gave her a warm hug. Eric, who had just been told that Fiona was very sad, asked her if she was all right. Fiona didn't say much. It seemed to me that she was exhausted and embarrassed. She pleaded with us to spend the night at Anthony's. After I had dropped her off, Tom and I hid all the medication that was in the house as instructed by the councillor and doctor.

We needed to watch her closely for the next few weeks. In her unstable state, she was not allowed to be on her own. I promised Tom that I would not leave her unsupervised in the house. And that I would drive her wherever she had to go.

That night, I cleaned the kitchen spotless. I mopped the floor, scrubbed pots, and reorganised shelves. Tom asked me if he should make teas for us. I nodded. After putting the kettle on, he gave me a hug.

I leaned my head against his shoulder and whispered, "You know, they say that suicidal behaviour is not uncommon amongst people with eating disorders, especially those who purge. This stupid illness is making her feel so worthless. I wish she were still a little kid. Helping her into her pyjamas when she was tired was so easy compared to this. I wish I could make her pain go away. Gosh, I feel so powerless."

"You're doing your best, darling," he said. "I'm so glad you didn't leave the bathroom."

"Me, too."

He kissed me and poured us tea. We didn't speak much after that. Tom took his tea to bed and read on his phone. I said good night to Winston, locked the front door, switched all the lights off downstairs and walked upstairs to sit on my yoga mat.

Exactly two years earlier, my mother had rung and told me that my brother had died.

"You know what he's like," she said. "He'd never go to the doctor. He'd self-diagnose, and this time I think he took the wrong medication. His heart stopped beating."

Then I heard her cry.

"The police had to break into his apartment. I'll call you tomorrow," she sobbed then hung up. None of that made any sense to me. For the rest of the day and all night, I had sat on my bed with my hands folded, tears pouring.

The following day my mother confirmed that he had taken his life. "He made a mistake," she said.

My brother had just returned from a two-week vacation in the States, and he was supposed to go to a concert with one of his best friends a few days later. I saw the tickets lying on the table when I stepped into his apartment. I also saw the filth and the mental pain. I saw the rigidity of a perfectionist and the loneliness of a genius brain.

We buried his ashes on a dull Thursday morning.

"It's this kind of weather that kills people," one of his colleagues said to me.

On that Friday, I visited his grave alone. I knelt in the wet grass and told him how sorry I was. I said it over and over again, that morning, and every single night when I revisited his apartment in my dreams. But with time passing, those dreams became less frequent.

Back then, Tom and I had decided not to disclose my brother's suicide to Eric and Fiona. It would put them at high risk, research said. They didn't need to know, not then, maybe later. Maybe never.

Now, I covered my face with trembling hands while my mind returned to my brother's one-bedroom apartment. I saw myself standing in a corner by the window surrounded by empty water bottles and piles of books. There was laundry drying on the back of a chair, and on the dusty floor a photo of Fiona and Eric in their school uniforms.

CHAPTER 7

Somebody who resembled my brother was trying to pick it up. He knelt down and then with the photo in his hand, lifted his face to mine, and gave me an angstful look.

"She's said she didn't want to end her life," I heard myself reassure him. "It was impulse. Believe me."

He nodded and disappeared.

Chapter 8

A week later, Anthony broke up with her. Despite all my love for him, I was pissed off. I mean, who in their right mind does something like this? After a year and a half of being together, he had waited for her to seriously contemplate suicide and then decided to leave her. In my self-talk, I accused him of being a selfish moppet who, too wrapped up in his own emotional bullshit, failed to see how dangerous the situation was. I lost all respect for him and Fiona's girlfriends, who, excited that Anthony was available again, were siding with him, leaving my daughter isolated and desperately lonely.

To my surprise, Fiona went to school and put on a brave face. She was fine, she said, brushing aside my attempts to console her. But was she really? I didn't trust her anymore. I knew she didn't want to burden me. Surely the eating-disorder voice would take advantage of this horrific situation. It would offer her an explanation for the breakup. Tell her that she was undesirable and fat.

And while the breakup was beyond Fiona's control, reducing her caloric intake wasn't. She had the option to distract herself and think about food instead of Anthony. She could restrict again or numb herself with a binge and then purge. She still had choices.

I would never find out why Anthony had changed his mind, but he reemerged in the middle of October at the scene of Tom's motorcycle accident, as if nothing had happened, when Fiona and I were standing at the edge of the windy country road about twenty minutes from our house watching the paramedics lift Tom's body into the ambulance. Tony put his arm around

CHAPTER 8

Fiona. She was crying silently. I was holding her hand. I was glad he was there.

The woman who had found Tom lying in the ditch had called me at home and told me to rush. When Fiona and I arrived, Tom was lying with his back on the ground, one leg awkwardly bent to the side. He was still conscious. I had temporarily lost my voice from the shock. After a few long moments, I managed to whisper his name. He hadn't heard me in his delirious state. *He could have been dead,* shot through my head, *or paralysed.*

"Your husband will be all right," one of the paramedics said to me and smiled. He was an attractive young man with powerful arms, who gave off such an air of confidence, it instantly lowered my heartbeat to a normal pace.

"We've given him horse tranquilliser," he laughed. "He's in Lala Land now. You can relax, he's not in pain anymore."

Then he disappeared into the back of the ambulance.

A policeman came out of nowhere and tapped me on the shoulder.

"You're his wife?" he asked. "Are you okay?"

I nodded stiffly. The officer walked away to talk to the ambulance driver.

Fiona, Anthony, and I embraced each other. Anthony tried to make a joke. We laughed nervously, looking into each other's eyes for comfort.

The paramedic reappeared. "We've checked his head," he said and ran his hand through his hair. "It's fine. He'll go straight into surgery for his fractures. Why don't you follow us to the hospital? You'll have the opportunity to speak with your husband before the doctor will knock him out again."

I wiped the tears off Fiona's face and pressed her body against my chest.

"Best I take you guys home real quick. When Eric returns from work, tell him that everything is okay. I don't want him to worry. Come on. Let's go! Daddy will be okay, Poppy, he's in good hands now."

Sweat was running down my back as I threw a random selection of shorts and T-shirts, Tom's toothbrush, razors, and underwear in a duffel bag, got back in the car, and raced to the hospital. *It looks like Anthony and Fiona are back together. His presence alone will console her,* I thought with relief while I ran along the seemingly endless hospital corridor to the emergency department.

The surgeon allowed me to take a seat next to Tom's bed. I wrapped my hands around his hand. He looked at me, scared, and mumbled something that didn't make much sense. I reassured him that I would be right by his side when he would wake up the following morning. With his eyes fixed on the X-rays, the physician informed me that Tom would need several surgeries, but he would walk again. Then he asked me to leave.

It was a hot evening. I rolled down the front windows, allowing fresh air to circulate as I drove along the empty road. Halfway home, my distress transformed into an enormous anger that lasted for weeks. *Life never seems to give my girl a break. A fair chance to sort out her mental troubles, that's all I'm asking for.* My foot tapped the accelerator. Should I have sent her to an eating disorder clinic where she could have been shielded from family, relationship, and friendship dramas? Or abroad, where she could have focused solely on her healing? Who would know the answer to that?

A while back, she had mentioned to me that she would never want to be put in an inpatient program. She said that amongst the competitive eating-disorder patients, it was all about who can be the skinniest and the most sick. Hearing another person talk about their weight loss always fuelled her eating disorder. And without a doubt, she would have missed Anthony and her dog if I had sent her away.

But not a day would go by without me thinking about how much the illness was costing her. Valuable adolescent years were lost to identifying as a bulimic. Now that life's circumstances were sending her into emotional spins, it coincided unfortunately with the challenges of her extreme hunger. The recovery process was dragging its feet, and our enthusiasm faded.

I tried to gather strength, sat up straight, threw my head back, and held the steering wheel as tightly as I possibly could. Like tropical rain, sudden floods of warm tears poured down my face. I had no idea how I was going to care for Fiona and Tom, who would be in a wheelchair for weeks after the operation, at the same time. Tomorrow, the hospital nurses would have to teach me how to give Tom blood-thinning injections to prevent thrombosis. In the afternoon, I would have to ring around to find a builder who could build a ramp up to Eric's apartment door at short notice. Tom would have to move into Eric's apartment, because it was on the ground floor, and Eric would move into our

CHAPTER 8

master bedroom. Eric had to work long hours, and I didn't want him to sleep on the sofa. *I'll have to exchange mattresses, clean and air his apartment. Oh, damn it, I never wanted Tom to own a motorcycle, but it's too late to get upset about that now. Tom is alive. That is all that matters.* I sighed and squinted my eyes. *Someone forgot to dim their headlights! So annoying!*

Tom was sitting propped up when Fiona and I entered the hospital room the following morning. The painkillers made him look almost cheerful.

"So glad they've been looking after you so well. You look good," I said and kissed his forehead. He smiled.

"Thank you for coming, Fiona," Tom said, looking at her, and then he joked about the large cuts on his legs where the doctors had inserted metal rods. He wanted to make her laugh, but she didn't. She didn't say anything, either. She just stared at his bandaged wrist.

Tom and I talked about the motorcycle.

"I'll pick it up tomorrow," I said. "The guy on the phone told me it's toast."

"Well, it's not like I'll be riding a motorcycle any time soon," Tom laughed. Then he asked me to push the nightstand a little closer to his bed so that he could reach his water and phone.

"What's this?" I pointed to a white plastic bag with clothes.

"You can throw them away," he said. "These are the clothes that the doctors had to cut into pieces to get off me."

I looked at Fiona. Her face was pale.

"I need to text work," Tom said.

"With one hand?" I asked.

"Sure," he said and leaned the cell phone against the pillow that was lying on his legs.

I sat down in a visitor chair. Tom started typing, but then the cell phone slid off the pillow and landed on the floor. As I bent down to scoop it up, I heard a loud bang. Something heavy had smashed on the floor on the other side of the bed. I raised my head and saw Tom press the emergency button. At once several nurses rushed into the room, all of them staring at Tom.

My eyes jumped to the floor. Fiona had collapsed!

I rushed around the bed and made sure her head wouldn't be lifted up too early because that's what they'd usually do. *Let her rest,* I thought. *This is all too much for my precious girl, and for me.* I knelt on the floor and stroked her head while the nurses helped her take a few sips of water. The fear for her father's life, or her undernourishment, or both, had caused anxieties responsible for her extreme body response.

Two days later, my suspicions that Fiona had not been eating enough were confirmed when Sally asked me to join in the last five minutes of the therapy session. Fiona revealed to both of us that she hadn't menstruated in almost one year. For crying out loud, not getting regular periods was a definite sign of her body still being undernourished. So, she had deceived Sally about doing well and eating enough. Or was she still unable to gage how much food her body needed? But didn't she say that she felt extreme hunger? She must give in to this extreme hunger. But how much was enough? I didn't know.

The only thing I knew was that she still didn't eat like a normal person. She was rigid in her choices, avoided cakes, chocolate, cream, anything with a large amount of fat or sugar in it. She never ate spontaneously. She never took a larger portion than the people she ate with.

From the very beginning, I had struggled with the well-meaning, yet vague instructions of the therapist. Feed her what everybody else in the family is eating. Don't make any exceptions for her. It had sounded so simple. Why then had I been so hesitant and indecisive? For a start, every one of us ate differently. Tom ate very little, but in the evenings after dinner, he had ice cream and wine. Eric never missed a second or third helping. My hunger varied from day to day. Sometimes I ate as little as Tom and sometimes as much as Eric.

And let's face it, didn't every household have different eating habits? My friend Olivia, for example, prepared three-course meals every day. She was into exotic recipes and desserts. Zara had a strict weekly rotation, with roast dinners every Sunday and fish and chips every Friday. She also loved to bake. Her normal snack was a cup of coffee and piece of cake in the afternoons. Alexa hated cooking. She wasn't a health nut, either. Her family subsisted on takeaways.

So, how much sour cream was I supposed to slap on nachos? One teaspoon or two? Was eating sour cream essential for recovery? Was a tuna sandwich for lunch enough? Did she need to have a yoghurt with her sandwich?

Your child should not be starving before the next meal, I read somewhere, but Fiona had said that she was. I suddenly doubted everything I did. I felt that I hadn't challenged the eating disorder as much as I should have. I thought it was my fault that Fiona wasn't recovered yet, and I was convinced that since she had been in control of her meals, she had given in to the eating disorder and restricted again. I was upset with the therapist. Why hadn't I been given a user-friendly manual with recovery meal plans for dummies and tick lists?

While Fiona slept for the rest of that day, I searched the Internet for hours until I discovered a parental guidebook for family-based therapy. It offered meal plans and precise portion sizes. *Why have I not come across this book before? Why hasn't the therapist told me that it exists? Could it be that she doesn't know?*

Hopeful, I downloaded the book, flopped on the sofa and began to read. The book didn't disappoint. I lost all sense of time, and when I got to the last page, I suddenly realised that it was 1 o'clock in the morning. With the weight of uncertainty lifted, I jumped up to make a tea and opened a packet of chocolate-chip cookies. Excited, I wanted to wake Fiona up, but her mind was currently processing the images of the accident scene. I had to wait. It would not be easy to persuade her of the need to fuel her body with more carbohydrates, because Dr. Stevens had told her that she wasn't sick anymore on the very day that Fiona had attempted to take an overdose. He had invited her to step on the scales. Coincidence? I doubted it.

"Routine," he had said and shrugged his shoulders. Then he had sat back at his desk and handed me a small piece of paper with her weight written on it, because Fiona had refused to know. Contently, he had smiled at her and asked how therapy was going. Fiona had said that she was improving.

"I'm happy to hear that. Seems like you're doing the right thing. According to the BMI you're not underweight."

It wasn't the first time I had heard this BMI nonsense. *We need a new breed of doctors,* I had thought and stood up, upset that Fiona had heard him. Although tempted, I knew better than to argue with the softhearted man Fiona confided in. Therefore, I had refrained from telling him that the BMI was nothing else but a ratio between height and weight. It was falsely believed to be an indicator of health. It didn't figure in people's genetics, their bone and muscle weight, or their lifestyle. I had explained this to Fiona, but her eating disorder was not prepared to acknowledge any of this.

Independent of the BMI, if the natural body weight was suppressed and the body starving, the female body simply couldn't afford to be losing blood every four weeks. But Dr. Stevens had, of course, never inquired about her period.

Two weeks after Tom's accident, I asked Fiona to come outside to get some vitamin D. The sun was shining. I was standing in my herb garden, pinching a few inches of the basil stems when Fiona tiptoed across the gravel to take a seat on the wooden bench by the rosemary bushes. I was pleasantly surprised to see her wearing a light blue T-shirt that looked reasonably tight on her. She watched me quietly. I could tell there was something on her mind.

"My gosh, the lemon balm has really gotten out of hand," I said to break the silence. I went to prune it back to an acceptable size. Then I gathered the stems and held them in front of Fiona's nose.

"Smell this," I said. "It's so yummy. We should take them inside and make tea with the leaves."

Fiona wrinkled her nose at me.

"Dad will be home tomorrow," I said.

"Sweet."

"I've been thinking that we should have our dinners in Eric's apartment for as long as Dad will have to stay down there. I don't want him to feel left out. We could sit around his bed and eat. What do you think?"

"Sounds good."

"Are you okay, Fiona?"

"Can we go inside?"

"Of course. Let me just finish watering. Here, take the lemon balm. I'll join you in a minute."

Fiona was already sitting on the sofa with her blanket wrapped around her for comfort, when I entered the kitchen, washed my hands, and turned to her.

"What's up?"

"I'm relapsing, Mummy."

She caught me off guard. I turned away from her and while I busied myself with gathering the lemon balm and putting them in a water filled jar, I swallowed my tears and cleared my throat.

"It's so hard to eat intuitively," she told me.

I tucked my T-shirt in, turned around, and walked over to her.

"Honestly, Poppy, why are you worried about eating intuitively?"

Fiona picked up her blanket and started to chew on one of the corners. I sat down beside her.

"Why do you say that you've relapsed?" I didn't bring myself to ask her if she was purging again. It felt like such an intimate question. I hoped that she would tell me what she meant by relapsing, but she didn't.

"I just have," she said.

"It happens," I said. "I guess we have to get you back on track. What do you think?"

I took her shy smile to be a yes and seized the opportunity to talk to her about the guidebook for family-based therapy with examples of meal plans and colourful photos of breakfasts, lunches, and dinners. Fiona moved closer to me. I was glad that she was interested. I reached for my iPad and brought up a photo of a large plate filled to the rim with chicken tikka masala, green beans, and rice. For long, curious moments, her usual irritability was gone, and she touched my arm affectionately. Perhaps she had also longed for prescription type meals with no leeway for mistakes.

"We've never put that much on my plate," she noticed.

"Exactly," I said.

While we studied the pages, she learnt that all her meals needed to contain the following food groups: proteins, starches, and fruit or vegetables, dairy, and definitively fat. Therefore, with each breakfast she should have a big glass of full-fat milk. For her lunch, she should have a sandwich with butter and cheese maybe, or a full-fat yoghurt. And in the evenings, she should have half her plate covered with something starchy, a quarter with protein and a quarter with vegetables. Meals should be prepared with avocado oil, butter, or have cream added. Both of us knew that Fiona had avoided full-fat milk, full-fat yoghurt, and mayonnaise. Secretly adding up calories, Fiona hadn't even gone near juices, claiming they contained too much sugar. But here was the thing with giving herself permission to eat: she couldn't have rules. Drinking apple juice was by all means a better choice than being stuck with an eating disorder that could lead to a premature death.

"Black coffee and water won't do the trick," I said. "Can you see that?"

"Yes," she said. "I'm happy you found this book. Maybe you could prepare whatever they suggest. I don't want to make any decisions around food for a while."

"You must get your period again," I said.

"I know."

"And you have to be honest with Sally," I urged her. "She's skilled, darling. But she can only get you out of this mess if you tell her the truth. The moment you lie, therapy becomes pointless, and it's costing Mum and Dad lots of money. Please don't waste this precious time that you have with her."

It took two people to get Tom home from hospital. One of his colleagues was more than happy to take a day off work and help me lift Tom's body in and out of the car seat and into the wheelchair. I had ordered comfortable foam pillows, cut flowers to brighten up the room, and brought a stack of library books home. But during the first week back, Tom didn't register any of this. He was in too much pain from the leg and wrist surgeries and too angry with himself about the accident.

The trauma had made him lose all tolerance for other people's needs. One minute he would thank me, and the next he would boss me around. I didn't respond, otherwise issues could have easily ended up in a street fight. We needed peace in this house where everybody was struggling with something.

Early in the mornings, I washed and dressed Tom. While he ate his breakfast, I quickly changed the sheets. Then I would go upstairs, prepare breakfast for Fiona, eat with her, make her school snack and lunch, stuff everything into her school bag, wait until she was dressed, and drop her off at school. While in town, I would go grocery shopping and visit the pharmacy.

CHAPTER 8

After returning home, I would keep Tom company. We would watch a movie or just talk, to take his mind off the pain. Then I would leave him to rest. At three o'clock, I would pick Fiona up from school and have a snack with her. I would cook dinner, dish out the food and place the plates on trays. I would add a glass of milk for Fiona. She and Eric would help me carry everything downstairs into his apartment, where we would eat with Tom. Then I'd instruct Eric and Fiona to do the dishes while I would help Tom go to the toilet, switch on the TV, adjust the pillows, give him his injection, hand him the TV remote, and switch off the lights. At nine o'clock, I would call Fiona for her snack. After that, I would hunker down on the sofa and relax, curled up in a blanket, until everybody was asleep.

Ever since Fiona had been diagnosed with bulimia, Eric had made sure that he blended in with the furniture when he came upstairs. I hardly spent time with him, but he didn't complain. It was convenient for me, but it wasn't fair on him. So, on the first Monday that Tom returned to work on crutches, Eric was on holiday, and I decided to go on a day hike with him. Fiona had borrowed my car to drive to school. Eric and I got our hiking boots on, packed a small backpack with sandwiches, water, and insect repellent, and drove to our destination in his car.

"We've got the perfect weather," I announced as we stepped out into the fresh air. Eric always talked when we walked. It was as if the vibrations from the movement loosened his facial muscles. He talked about his work mates, and then we talked about Fiona.

"Why does she get herself into so much trouble?" he asked, crossing a shallow river.

"A mental illness is difficult to explain," I replied. "She doesn't choose to."

"She should stop worrying about what other people think."

"Yes, I wish she could do that."

After a short climb, we descended into an area with mangroves. We stopped at a clearing in the mangrove swamp and sat down to eat our packed lunch. I took my shoes off and stuck my feet in the turquoise water.

"I'm sorry for not having spent much time with you," I began. "All I can think of is making sure your sister gets better."

"It's okay." He picked up a pebble and threw it as far as he could. "Not sure if you can help her," he added.

"Let's hope I can," I replied.

It was early afternoon when we returned to the car park. We had been out of reception for several hours. I quickly checked my phone for messages. Happy to see that I hadn't received any, I sat down in the passenger seat and changed into my beach sandals. "I really enjoyed today. So nice doing something different."

Eric nodded. He started the car. My phone rang. It was Fiona. I placed my phone on my lap and put her on speaker.

"Mum, I'm having a meltdown. I'm leaving school to go home."

"Fiona, don't!" I shouted. "Please! Nobody's at home. Eric and I have finished the hike, we're on our way, but it will take us two hours before we're back in town."

"I'm not staying in school."

"You have to, please, Fiona, this one time," I continued to shout. What was the problem? She had been going to school just fine for the last two weeks. The one day I was out with Eric! I couldn't believe this was happening. Was she doing it on purpose?

"I can't," she said.

"You're not allowed to be home alone," I said in a stern voice. "Under no circumstances."

"I'll go to Anthony's then."

"His mum works, and there will be nobody in the house."

"I'll get him out of class. He'll only miss last period."

Luckily, I knew that Anthony's mother wouldn't mind.

"Okay, then. Promise?"

"Yes."

When Eric and I got into town, we stopped at Anthony's. Fiona opened the front door. I was relieved that she was safe.

Seven weeks already had passed since the accident, and Tom was healing well. Fiona had followed my suggestion and befriended Joe and Carl. I was gaining confidence in preparing suitable meals for Fiona. After one of those meals, Fiona suddenly complained about a fever and a sore throat. She had caught tonsillitis, and during the week that followed, she could barely swallow anything. It was the second time that she was sick with tonsillitis this year. Disillusioned, I saw us backtrack with her nutritional rehabilitation. Rather than serving her big meals, I would sit perched on the edge of Fiona's bed and watch her suck on ice cubes.

Sometimes I would doze off. One afternoon, she woke me up pulling my hand.

"I never want to eat more than my friends when we go out together," she said. It was crazy how repetitive her thoughts were. We had talked about this so many times already.

"Remember that this thought doesn't make any sense," I said, "because you can't possibly know what your friends ate beforehand and what their metabolisms are like."

Of course, she knew all of this.

"You know, sometimes when I sit in class, I suddenly feel fat and then I can't think of anything else," she said after a while.

"Fat is not a feeling. Like fat people don't feel fat. They might say about themselves that they're fat, but they don't feel fat."

"But I feel fat when I'm upset," she said.

"You have to practice labelling your emotions correctly. Stop using the word fat for everything."

The next day I bought Fiona a journal. I encouraged her to write down these limiting beliefs. It is easier to analyse them when you can actually see them on paper, I explained. Irrational thoughts are rigid, but not unshakeable.

It happened on a weekend. Eric and Tom were asleep, Fiona was at Anthony's, and I was sitting with my laptop at the kitchen table reading about a promising Mexican company that was traded on the US stock market. While I submitted a market order that bought me twenty shares, I suddenly remembered that I had hardly eaten anything all day. I got up and opened the fridge door hoping to find hummus and Spanish olives.

A car pulled up the driveway. Before I had the time to get to the window to check who was coming to visit at this late hour, I heard doors being slammed, and then I heard Fiona wailing like I had never heard her before. I rushed into her bedroom and saw her lying in bed with a fleece blanket pulled over her head.

"What's happened?" I asked, concerned.

She said something, but all I heard through her muffled sobs was Anthony's name.

"What's up with Anthony?" I asked. "Is he okay?" When I stepped forward to lean over her, I almost crushed the phone that she had thrown on the floor.

"He's broken up with me for good," she bawled.

"Oh, boy, I'm so sorry." I gently lifted the blanket to see her face, but she tore it out of my hand and pulled it back over her head.

"Can I do something for you?" I asked. "Would you like to talk, or do you want me to make you a tea? I can just sit with you, if you like."

"I want to be alone, Mum."

I stopped in the doorway of her bedroom, but then I left her and returned to the kitchen, my mouth dry. I took my phone off the table trying to keep my hands still. Then I walked upstairs with the plan to do nothing. I sat on a beanbag and listened to Fiona's crying. Breakups were so hard. She cared so much for Anthony. I felt tired. I wanted to go to bed, but I waited until Fiona's crying had subsided.

A text message showed up on my phone. It was from Anthony.

R u still awake? Can u please go and check on Fiona?

I bolted downstairs and opened her bedroom door. She was a trembling lump under the blanket, with only her face and one arm sticking out. Her face was swollen and wet with tears. The arm was dangling down the side of her bed holding the phone in her hand.

"Mummy, Mummy, Mummy," she cried.

My eyes wandered over to her nightstand. I saw several empty pill packages bent and scattered. Hastily I switched on the lights.

"Fiona, what have you done?"

"I took my pill, I mean, all of them, the whole pack," she wept. "I'm so

CHAPTER 8

scared."

You can't kill yourself with an overdose of the contraceptive pill. Oh, what a stupid girl she is! Or maybe you can? Fuck, nobody prepared me for this. Why did I even want to become a mother? I could be sitting under a palm tree right now with my childless friend, Lola, sipping on a piña colada. Well, I better act fast. We need to get to hospital before it's too late.

Fiona's face paled. She sat up, still crying with fear.

"Darling, calm down. Let me call an ambulance. In the meantime, put your shoes on and grab a sweatshirt. You have to go to hospital."

I ran into the lounge, lifted the phone, and dialled emergency services.

"I'm sorry, but we can't send an ambulance. All our vehicles are out," a male voice said.

Without responding, I hung up and ran upstairs to wake Tom.

"Quick, get dressed. Fiona took an overdose of her pill. We must drive her to hospital. I can't get an ambulance. I will try one more time while you're getting ready."

My heart was pounding. I ran downstairs and dialled 911 again.

"Can you please tell me how long the wait will be?" I shouted.

"No sorry, I can't," said the male voice from earlier.

"What if my daughter dies?"

"It's best you drive to hospital in your own car."

"If she dies on the way, then it's your fault," I yelled and slammed the receiver on the hook, aware that I was losing control. Tom was equally stressed, but he took it out on Fiona. He entered Fiona's room and threw his crutches on the ground, hissing that she should stop texting. He ripped the mobile out of her hand. I rushed into the bedroom to defer the escalating situation.

"Let's go. You drive, Tom."

I escorted Fiona out of the house and scooted next to her on the backseat. "You'll be all right," I whispered in her ear. "Let me call the emergency services again."

"I'm so scared."

"Sir, could you please connect me with the hospital. I would like to talk to a nurse," I pleaded into my phone.

I was worried Fiona would vomit or go unconscious. The nurse reassured me that Fiona would be okay, and most likely she wouldn't throw up.

"We'll be ready for her when you get here," she said, quite matter of fact as if confirming a hairdresser's appointment.

I kissed Fiona's head. Her wet hair stuck to my naked arm as she leaned against my shoulder. Carefully, I listened to her breathing.

Two nurses in dark blue scrubs received us. One of them took Fiona's arm and guided her away from me into another room. The other nurse told Tom and me to wait, then disappeared. We sat down across from each other on the unfriendly white paper sheets that cover hospital beds.

"Attention seeking," Tom said, annoyed, "and I have to work tomorrow."

"Are you for real?" I was infuriated. "How dare you say that?! And how dare you say that to her. Work! I don't think you get what just happened. What if she had taken something that could have killed her? A suicide attempt is not attention seeking. And I heard you say that to her while I was on the phone. Now you've convinced her that she is a burden. For heaven's sake! And why did you throw your damn crutches on her bedroom floor? Why do you always have to be like that, make things worse?"

Immense silence. Tom stared at the floor.

"And by the way, where's Fiona's phone? You had no reason to take it off her. Give it to me."

Before Tom could react, a young nurse appeared in the door frame. I started to feel uncomfortable and lowered my eyes. After all, I was the mother of someone who thought that there was no reason for living. Without a doubt, she was judging me despite her charming smile. It was all too obvious that I had failed at protecting my daughter from thoughts of purposelessness, from feeling trapped. I was ashamed. I quietly answered her questions when she interviewed me about the course of events.

"She's suffering from bulimia," I added, as if this would explain everything.

"She told us," the nurse said. "Well, her stomach is fine, and she seems stable. You may go home now, but we'll keep her for the night. That's how it is with suicide attempts."

CHAPTER 8

I sighed, feeling strangely liberated. I wouldn't have had the strength to look after Fiona that night. She was safe in hospital, and I needed reliable silence. Back home in bed, I lay awake for half the night, wondering if it was true that I couldn't help Fiona, just like my son had said.

"Where is my phone?" That's how she greeted me the following morning. She was sitting upright, dressed in her bed, ready to leave. I felt insanely betrayed. While I worried about her life, she worried about her phone.

I fixed my eyes on hers and with a kind, but firm voice, said, "I don't know. Dad has it. You'll get it back when he gets home. Now, we need to talk about what we can do so that these things don't happen again."

"I'm sorry."

"That's okay," I said.

The physician entered the room. She observed how chirpy Fiona looked and said that she could be discharged. Oh, and by the way, it would help if we stopped by the public health nurse for a session on our way home, she suggested.

"It's something we need to get signed off," the doctor said.

I was gobsmacked. So, that was it? The ear, nose and throat specialist had treated Fiona's recurring tonsillitis with more seriousness than this doctor treated her suicide attempt. And nobody seemed to care about me. Parents were expected to cope with anything.

In my desperation, I turned to Winston for support. He was delighted to see Fiona and immediately skipped onto her bed when she came home. *His affection will ease her psychological pain*, I thought. I made sure that he didn't leave her side for the next few days. And when night came, she would hug him tightly and listen to his reassuring heartbeat.

The school holidays had started, and I tried my hardest to keep Fiona socially integrated and busy. During the first week, I rented two large cabins, and we invited eight students from her year group to spend a couple of nights at the beach with us. Fiona went swimming several times a day. She joined in the ball games and stayed up until late in the night chatting. To an outsider, it looked as if Fiona was part of the action, but much later she told me that she had not ever been fully present.

Unfortunately, she was unable to hold a summer job because of her mood swings and fatigue. I asked her to structure her days in other ways. She planned to go on short walks in the mornings, to spend time with Winston, to go shopping with me, and to go to the gym. But Instagram showed her unwanted photos of weekend parties to which she was not invited. The photos depleted her of the energy that she needed to stick to her daily routine.

Two days before Christmas, Leila spread false rumours about Fiona. She bullied her online. Fiona fell sick again. For the third time, she had tonsillitis. She was booked in for having her tonsils removed after Christmas.

Then one afternoon, I heard her laugh. I halted in my tracks. She was in her room with the door half open. Who was she talking to? She laughed again. An old friend from the States maybe? I tried to eavesdrop from where I stood in the lounge, but all I picked up were screeches, snorts, and snickers. Eventually, she came running into the lounge, clutching her belly and gasping for air.

"Guess what?"

"Yeah?"

"I just talked to Sabrina."

"Oh, really? That's fantastic. How is she? Is she still in Christchurch?"

"No, she's moving with her family to Auckland in two days, and she has invited me to move in with her."

"Hold on, slowly."

"She said that in their new house, they'll have a spare room for me. Sabrina and I could go to the local high school together. She's a bit anxious about moving without knowing anybody. With me there, she wouldn't be so alone."

"I'm not so sure about this plan. What about her mum and dad? She would have to ask them first, don't you think?"

"Could you talk to her mum? Oh, pleeeaase! Her parents are fine with it."

"You're hoping."

"No, Sabrina already asked while we were talking. Remember, they really like me."

CHAPTER 8

"I do."

"It would make me so happy. Please, Mum. I want to move to Auckland."

"We'll have to think this through really carefully before I even call her mother."

After dinner, I shared the news with Tom.

"No. She's not going," he said. "She is too unstable. It won't work."

"I hear what you're saying. It might not turn out well, and she might not stay long, but I think she should try. I know that mental problems stay with you, even when you change your environment, but perhaps she can get better with the support of a real girlfriend." I paused, and then I said, "She has nobody here, Tom. And some people say that you cannot heal in the same environment you got sick in."

"Whatever. I'm against it."

"Can I talk to Sabrina's mum and Sally, see what they say, and then we decide?"

"You do whatever."

Later that evening, Fiona told me that she would be so motivated to eat everything without restriction if she could go. She said that here, our slick kitchen countertops, the gas stove, the wooden surface of the dining table, the chairs, the fridge and the pantry doors, everything reminded her of food restriction and binge eating. The bathroom reminded her of purging. Her desire to wipe everything from her memory and to make a fresh start was fierce.

I could relate to everything she said, perhaps because I was secretly wishing to make a fresh start myself. When it was my turn to speak, I shared with her my concerns and conditions. I told her that Sabrina's family would not be responsible for monitoring her eating disorder.

"That would be an impossible ask," I said, and she got it.

She alone would be in charge, and if she slipped back, she would have to come home. Deep inside, though, I had an uneasy feeling when I called Sabrina's mother the next day. I let her know that Fiona had been struggling with bulimia, and while she didn't binge and purge anymore and was eating quite well lately, there was the possibility that she would restrict again and that's when she would have to return home.

Sabrina's mother was not worried about Fiona's bulimia; in fact, she was delighted about the prospect of having her around because Sabrina had been suffering from mild depression and really needed a friend. Perhaps both could uplift each other.

I inquired about the family's eating habits. She said that Sabrina and her two sisters would make their own breakfast—usually scrambled eggs and toast plus a glass of juice or milk—then they would put together their school lunches, and in the evenings, she would cook dinner. The family would eat together, and yes, dessert was non-negotiable. I knew that Sabrina and her sisters were good eaters and believed that their household wasn't a fat-shaming one with lots of rules around food. *Maybe this could work after all?* I became hopeful.

I called Sabrina's mother a few more times to chat about this and that. Eventually, when it was clear that Fiona would move to Auckland for her last year of high school, she welcomed every morning by opening her bedroom curtains. At last, sun rays would enter her small dark world. Then she would skip into the kitchen to eat a huge breakfast. Later in the day, she would sit on her bed and call Sabrina. For hours, she would giggle and gasp and laugh.

And I would stand in the hallway and listen.

Chapter 9

From the moment Fiona and I entered their home on our first day in Auckland, Sabrina's family included us in conversations about aunts, cousins, and neighbours as if we were family.

There were nice people, Brian and Vanessa. She was a few years younger than me: pretty, with straight, blonde, shoulder-length hair loosely tied up in a relaxed loop at the back of her neck. The hairstyle complimented the tight jeans and dark blue T-shirt she wore every day, and in which she moved around with an easy grace. After I had spent about a week with her, I found her energy to be never ending, especially when it came to carting the girls to netball training, birthday parties, family get-togethers, and fundraisers. I could see how much she enjoyed participating in her daughters' activities, and I trusted her to look after Fiona.

Brian was a rugged-looking man with an unintentional three-day stubble beard and a solid sense of humour. His arms looked tough as if they had lifted fence posts all their lives, and his firm beer gut was controlled and likeable. His speech matched his looks: rough around the edges, but he never quite meant it that way. He also had a softer side. One evening, I had watched him mediate a fight between Sabrina's younger sisters as if it were nothing. Ten-year-old Hazel had whacked her twelve-year-old sister, Laura, with a bag of frozen chips. Laura screamed on the top of her lungs, threatening to break one of Hazel's toys in retaliation. Unperturbed, he sat both girls down and chatted through things. A few moments later, I saw Hazel apologising to Laura and disappearing behind her bedroom door, into what I guessed was time out, while Vanessa was flicking through a magazine with her feet resting on an ottoman. She didn't even look up.

As instructed by Sally, who had supported Fiona's move and equipped her with coping strategies, I refrained from talking about the intricacies of bulimia with Sabrina's family, but I was open about Fiona needing occasional encouragement to eat the same foods as everybody else. We were gathered around the four-meter-long dining table, scraping the last bits of Brian's special shrimp sauce off our plates, when I brought it up. "Sometimes she doesn't like to eat dessert."

I sat next to Hazel, who gawked at me in disbelief.

"You have to make sure she doesn't skip it," I added and glanced at her.

"But dessert is the best!" Hazel exclaimed, tapping her little index finger on Fiona's arm like a woodpecker, as if this would prove her point.

"I'll make sure she eats her dessert," she said with determination, then she pushed her perfectly round, blue-rimmed glasses all the way up until they touched her forehead. "And if you're lucky, Fiouunaaa, I'll sneak you a double portion." She grinned.

"No, Hazel, a normal-sized portion is okay," I said, surprised to see my daughter chuckle. Maybe this little kid could teach her to lose her fear of sweet foods.

"Don't you like ice cream or jelly slices?" Hazel asked Fiona.

"Or pineapple lumps?" tooted Laura.

"No, of course, I do ..." Fiona responded, not flustered by the question.

"See?!" Hazel declared triumphantly, then she burped out loud with her mouth wide open and made us all laugh.

Not long after dinner, the four girls jumped into the heated pool for an evening swim. Brian took care of the messy kitchen, and Vanessa poured us each a glass of perfectly chilled white wine. We both sank into the leather couches from where we had a view of the illuminated Skytower. I felt envious of Fiona's new residence.

"We've got a bed for you, if you want another wine," Vanessa offered and then she returned to the conversation about food. "Friday nights we get takeaways," she said, as if apologising.

CHAPTER 9

"Perfect," I uttered. "Look, Vanessa, please don't think that you have to do anything different for Fiona. She'll eat whatever you guys are eating. The only thing is that she can't skip meals. She also needs to eat her snacks at regular intervals, but hey, she can take care of that herself. She's brought the container she keeps her snacks in, and she has stored it on one of the top shelves in your pantry. Please, don't worry about her eating, really."

"I'm so glad she's here," Vanessa said. "I've found Sabrina's depressive mood frustrating."

"Yes, the two are so happy together. What a saving grace."

"You know, back in our old place, Sabrina would lock herself into her bedroom every other day after school. This is how bad it had gotten. She was unhappy about moving, but also the competition amongst the girls in her year group was wearing her out. All this social media stuff. Brian came close to flushing her phone down the toilet." She laughed, and I smiled at her.

"I'm grateful that Fiona has the opportunity to live with you and Brian," I said. "Our house is too quiet sometimes. It was different when Tony came around."

Vanessa nodded. She understood.

"And Fiona gets bored so easily. It's hard for me to entertain her. She'll enjoy being part of your big family."

"This place sure gets loud. I hope Hazel and Laura won't annoy her too much."

"Oh, there's one other thing," I said changing the subject slightly. "Every second Thursday, Fiona has a Skype therapy session with her eating disorder specialist. The sessions are an hour long. She usually shuts herself in her bedroom, and it would be good if nobody disturbed her during that time."

"Not a problem. Most Thursday afternoons I'm out with the little girls, visiting my mother."

As far as I could tell, nothing seemed to be a big deal in this household. Later that night, when I knocked on Fiona's bedroom door to say good night, I found her and Sabrina in sleeping bags on the bedroom deck listening to music and gazing at the stars.

"What a lovely setup," I said, and she smiled proudly.

As I walked down the long hallway back into the living room, I noted that Vanessa and Brian's house was not only significantly larger than ours, it also smelled of sweet, cut flowers and apple-spiced candles. I was happy for Fiona. Here she would be able to make a fresh start with lots of room for constructive thoughts. And she would meet girls her age who would have no idea that she was recovering from bulimia.

And perhaps she would be able to forget Anthony and fall in love with someone else. It was the beginning of Fiona restoring her old self, I believed, though I knew I could be wrong.

I had planned to give Vanessa the time and space to organise her younger girls for their first week back at school. Therefore, I told Sabrina and Fiona that I would take them out for a walk along the viaduct and on a ferry ride.

"Why don't you guys make a packed lunch?" I suggested. "It'll save us money. Don't worry about me. I've bought myself a sandwich on the way."

From where I sat on the deck, I could see Sabrina open the double-door fridge, which I swore must have been a special-order appliance. It was huge and packed with food as if it stood in a restaurant kitchen. She pulled out an armful of items and let them slide onto the countertop. Fiona emerged from the walk-in pantry with a can of tuna, spooned some of its contents on a slice of bread, topped it with lettuce leaves, and told Sabrina, who had pushed the mayonnaise jar over to her, that she wasn't really into mayonnaise.

As soon as both of them had their sandwiches, apples, and water bottles packed, we set off. First, we walked along K Street to browse through thrift stores. I bought a long-sleeved corduroy top because both girls insisted that I looked great in it.

"Like a true hippie, aye, Mum?" Fiona teased me.

My eyes crinkled in amusement. I enjoyed her good mood. Then we headed for the harbour. I bought us ice creams. Fiona ate only the top half of hers, the other half she chucked in a street bin, claiming that the flavours that she had chosen tasted disgusting.

At around five thirty, we returned to our Auckland homestead. The girls rushed down the hallway into Fiona's bedroom.

CHAPTER 9

I sank into one of the couches and put my feet up.

Vanessa came into the living room wearing a bathrobe.

"I just went for a dip in the pool. What a hot day! How was it? Did you guys have fun?"

"Yes, the girls had a blast. They talked about going out together on the weekends."

"Now that both can drive and they have each other, there will be plenty for them to do. They won't get bored, believe me."

After a few moments of content silence, we grumbled about the extortionate prices of school uniforms and discussed which sports the girls might want to enrol in.

"Fiona said she'd be keen—" I started when roaring laughter interrupted me. Fiona and Sabrina barged into the room. Both looked stunning in their tight jeans and corset-type tops. Sabrina wore heavy makeup whereas Fiona wore only a light touch of mascara. However, the glamour of their outfits spread a momentary confusion, because normally they would wear comfortable track pants in the house.

"We're heading out," Sabrina clarified.

"Already?" I asked.

"Yes, we're meeting up with those girls who will be in our year group," Fiona snapped. "We've told you this. The ones we've connected with on Instagram."

"And where exactly are you going?" Vanessa didn't sound pleased either.

"Just to this place by the mall, and then to a party at this girl Karla's place next door."

"You haven't had any dinner yet," I said. The fact that I needed to remind her in front of Vanessa irritated me to no end.

"I'll make some macaroni and cheese," Vanessa said and jumped up.

"No, you sit down, Vanessa," I insisted feeling guilty for chasing her up. "I'll make them something real quick."

"No," Sabrina said turning to her mother. "We have to go *now*."

"Text the girls that you'll be twenty minutes late," I said. "You both need to eat something."

"We'll get something at the fast food place down the road." Fiona looked away when she spoke.

"What are you getting?" I asked.

"A wrap," she improvised, and her words sounded muffled.

By that point I didn't have the energy to care anymore. I knew that Sabrina, in contrast to her, was going to eat a complete meal, burger, fries and a soft drink, but I wasn't going to say that to Fiona in front of Vanessa.

Devastated and powerless, I drove to my hotel room not long after the girls had left, under the false pretence that I still had a few hours of online work to do.

It was early evening when I crossed the lobby of the airport hotel, recoiling at the thought of having to greet other guests. Luckily, I found the area in front of the elevators deserted and, in my haste to get to my room, I pressed several buttons at once. With my arms folded around my waist, I waited. The bell of an arriving elevator made me briefly raise my head. I stepped into the empty lift that would take me to the second floor, clutched the metal handrail, and shut my twitchy eyes. I felt nauseous from the abrupt upward pull. My room was the cheap one, at the very end of the narrow hallway. The one with a view of dumpsters.

Once inside the room, I turned around to shut out reality with a hopeful push, but the heavy door took its own time in closing. Involuntarily, I shuffled across the room and fell face first onto the mattress. My arms hugged the pillow. I noticed an unpleasant smell of bleach. Then, at long last, I wailed and mourned like never before, my body giving in to a monumental sadness. Two hours later, enveloped by a growing darkness, my body still shivered. I knew I had no more strength left. To soothe myself I hummed like a baby. It was eleven o'clock when I searched for my phone to text Fiona that I wasn't coming to see her the following day. *I'll come the day after for dinner*, I wrote. It would be my last night of the ten days that I had been staying in Auckland, and I had promised to cook for Sabrina's family.

Mum, please, come tomorrow. What's up? she texted back.

You're restricting, Fiona. I know you are. I'm not dumb. And maybe you only

CHAPTER 9

came here for that reason. I'm done. I can't play this game anymore. I need a day by myself. I'm not coming tomorrow.

It took a few lengthy moments before she responded.

I'm not restricting. I know how important it is for me to eat. Please come, Mummy. I love you so much.

Without texting back, I shut my phone off. Exhausted, I crawled back into bed, rolled up the duvet and hugged it as if it were a person. Then I whimpered until long after midnight, when I finally fell into a dreamless, comatose sleep out of which I awoke the next morning feeling inert and numb.

Although it was an overcast day, normal for Auckland summer, I wore sunglasses. Aimlessly, I wandered through a mall about a ten-minute drive from the airport, with my phone still switched off. After half an hour or so, I entered a coffee shop to comfort myself with a crunchy lemon muffin and triple-shot mocha. My legs felt heavy this morning. I touched my face. It was still hot and far too swollen to wear makeup. I took the plate with the warm muffin to an armchair by the window, sat down and I looked around. I saw middle-aged men and women getting out of their cars and lining up at the counter to order takeaway coffees. I could smell their perfumes and aftershaves. All of them were smartly dressed and purposeful. I let my hands glide over my wrinkled dress. *Did I wear this the day before?* I couldn't remember. My mocha arrived.

A backpack smashed against the window. My eyes flinched. Two teenage girls in larger bodies than Fiona's caught my attention. Both were happily laughing as they playfully pushed each other.

I touched the rim of the hot mug with the tip of my fingers. For over a year, I had stood by Fiona, unwavering. In conversations with the dean, therapist, councillor, physician, Tom, and Anthony, I had pleaded, explained, negotiated, and rectified. Every time that Fiona had lashed out at me, shouted, slammed doors, or pushed me away, I had forgiven her. Never had my touch, when given permission to stroke her or to wrap her in blankets, lost its compassion.

I had moved her to Auckland, enrolled her at the local medical centre, visited her new school to introduce us both to the teachers and dean. I had made sure that she felt comfortable in Sabrina's home, had paid board for her stay, and had given her my car for the year. I had done all of this without hesitation and without expectation.

So, why did I all of a sudden feel so hurt? So used? Why did I think of her as a liar? A manipulator? Someone who only pretended that they wanted to get over their mental illness?

Whatever the reason, when I had heard her fabricate arguments for eating less than Sabrina earlier that day, something inside me had snapped.

When osteoporosis hits her in her late fifties, I won't be alive anymore. The health issues she'll have at my age will be entirely her problem.

For the first time since her diagnosis, I was prepared to throw in the towel. I had expected her to be grateful and appreciative. We had involved other people. Sabrina's parents, Vanessa and Brian, had gone out of their way to decorate her bedroom and to make her feel welcome. And Sabrina was expecting her to stay for the year, but I already knew she wouldn't. The whole situation felt like the dry piece of muffin that was stuck in my throat, only that it wasn't quite as easy as taking a huge gulp of mocha to wash it down.

On my last evening in Auckland, it thunderstormed. I rushed to bring my shopping bags inside. Despite the terrible weather, Brian had been sitting on the covered deck, where he sipped on a beer in a can. When he heard me enter the house, he came inside and went to grab a towel so that I could dry myself off. He called to Vanessa, who was at the other end of the house with Hazel and Laura. "Honey, do you need me to help? Fiona's mum is here."

"All good, darling," she shouted. "We're almost done in the bath."

With interest, Brian watched me unpack jars of sauerkraut, sausages, and pickled gherkins. As always, he offered me a drink, and then he wandered around the house whistling to country music, mostly out of tune, while I peeled potatoes.

Sabrina and Fiona came into the kitchen.

"Hi, Mum," Fiona said cheerfully as if nothing had happened. I looked down at her feet as I gave her a fleeting hug. "Mum's making German potato salad," she said to Sabrina. "You're going to love it. Everybody loves it."

CHAPTER 9

Dinner was ready at seven. I kept my eyes fixed on Hazel and Laura, who loved the foreign food and didn't hesitate to take second and third helpings. Brian inquired about the recipe, then the conversation turned to the Auckland housing market. Sabrina's parents were looking to buy a house. They liked the house they were in, they said, and they were hoping to purchase it.

"Brian is going to meet with the owners tomorrow," Vanessa said. "Maybe we can get a deal if we don't have to involve a real estate agent."

"That would be fantastic," I said.

Sabrina and Fiona stood up and excused themselves from the table.

Before they were able to disappear down the hallway, Laura shouted, "They have to do the dishes tonight. Me and Dad did them last night."

"We'll come back when you guys are done," Sabrina replied.

"Would you like a gin and tonic?" Vanessa offered me.

I declined politely. "Actually, I might have a cup of tea instead if you don't mind, and then I'll have an early night."

"What time is your flight tomorrow morning?"

"Eleven."

The way Vanessa and I stood at the kitchen counter holding mugs of warm tea attested to how close we had become over the last two weeks.

"I hope you'll be all right," she said and put her hand on my shoulder. "I know you'll miss her terribly."

I wasn't quite sure if I agreed with her that night. The next morning, just before I boarded the plane, I turned my head one last time. I had hugged Fiona goodbye and now I saw her and Sabrina walking away, arm in arm, like sisters. I swallowed and told myself to be brave, looked to the front, and continued on my way to the passenger-boarding bridge. I had wanted her to have this opportunity. Nevertheless, the time that Fiona and I had spent together since her diagnosis had been so intense that it felt as if I were leaving a part of me behind.

Several hours later, when I was back home and resting on my bed, I received a bunch of photos from Vanessa. *She must have taken all the girls to the beach this afternoon,* I thought, looking at the four of them posing like celebrities. The last photo she sent was of Fiona on her own. Her cheeks were rosy, and the dark circles under her eyes were gone. Her smile was blissful and radiated content. She wore my dark purple sweater, which made her contrasting green eyes shine like emeralds. She looked gorgeous. Over the next weeks, I fiercely held on to the photo as a token of her happiness. But this was the problem with caring for someone who suffered from bulimia.

Although Fiona looked joyful, one was never quite sure if the eating disorder was standing at the back door with a big grin.

The next two weeks passed quickly. Then, one Monday on a perfect late summer afternoon, Anthony called. He asked me if he could take Winston for a walk to the beach. He said he was missing the fluff ball. The water in the bay was warm, and Winston had us in stitches because he couldn't stand being wet. Every time he came out of the water, he shook his entire body so rigorously, we thought his fur would fly off, and his legs would bend like matchsticks.

"What a silly dog you are," I said, "as if the water hurts your skin or something. Go for a run with Tony. Come on, I bet he'll tire you out."

I sat down while they ran, let the sand glide through my fingers, and stared at the horizon. I missed Fiona. And I kind of missed Anthony and Fiona being together.

But on the drive up to Auckland, Fiona had told me that Anthony had cheated on her. I knew Fiona was hurt. The relationship had been what they would call a toxic one for some time. Anthony had become very jealous whenever she talked with other boys at a party, and several times he had caused a scene, she had explained. Since the first breakup, they had argued a lot. Yet, Anthony had been like my second son. I had a soft spot for him. In my eyes, he had rescued my daughter. I would never forget that.

On the way back into town, we stopped for fish and chips. I tied Winston to one of the outdoor tables in the parking lot and poured water in his bowl, while Anthony picked up our order. He unwrapped the greasy lemon fish and the salty chips and asked me if I wanted tomato sauce.

"You mean ketchup?"

"No, Mamma, we're in New Zealand."

CHAPTER 9

"Don't be cheeky!"

He smiled, but then his face turned serious, and he asked, "Have you heard from Fiona?"

"Yes, I have."

"How do you think she is? I called her yesterday, but she didn't say much. Sabrina is always in the background. They giggle the whole time. It's so annoying. I don't know. I cannot really talk to her anymore. She's so different now," he lamented.

"Mm-hmm, I hear you, Tony. Whenever I call her, it's the same. But, you see, she's really had a tough time here. I won't mention any names, you know who I mean anyway. The girls here are bitches, and some of the guys are, too. All acting like big fish in a small pond. It's so nice for her to finally have a girlfriend she can have fun with and actually trust. She'll be able to be herself."

Anthony nodded hesitantly, not quite convinced by what I had said. "I miss her," he muttered. "It's such a long time until Easter."

"Only eight more weeks," I said and turned my face away from him.

As soon as I arrived at home, I rinsed the beach sand off my feet, and threw my towel in the wash, when Olivia dropped by unexpectedly.

That's rare, I thought, *but I'm glad.* Tom was in Christchurch for a business meeting, Eric was back on night shift, and I was longing for company. Before we settled on the balcony, I made us lemonades with crushed ginger and mint.

"So, how does it feel, not having Fiona around?" Olivia took a sip of her drink. "Yummy, I'm loving these."

"They are good, aren't they?"

"Back to my question ..." she started.

"It's different, now that it's just Tom and me upstairs."

"You both must be enjoying the break."

I stirred my lemonade for much longer than I needed. Eventually I said, "To tell you the truth, it feels odd. We don't have much to say to each other. I think during this last year, we have only ever talked about Fiona."

"You look exhausted."

"I shouldn't really, I've just come back from the beach. I took Winston and

Tony with me."

"Tony?"

"Yes, Tony. I think he and Fiona haven't completely split up."

"Oh, that's no good. Hmmm. How is she, anyway?"

"She sounds really happy on the phone," I said. "She likes the big city, and although she was a bit anxious at first, she is driving around quite a bit. She and Sabrina have made new friends, and they are invited to lots of parties. She's finally catching up on lost time."

"Does she like her new teachers?" Olivia asked.

"Yes. I think it was a good thing she left."

"There's so much more to do in Auckland than here in this tiny town. When is she turning eighteen?"

"In May."

"I'm glad you're getting a break." Olivia put her lemonade on the floor and touched my elbow.

"Yes, me too. I didn't realise how much I needed it. For months, I have been on alert. Now I sleep so much."

"You and Tom should do something nice, go somewhere ..."

I looked Olivia straight in the eyes and said, "I'm not interested."

She paused. "What are you trying to say?"

"Not sure."

"Where's Tom, anyway?"

"He's in Christchurch for two nights," I told her. I walked into the kitchen to fix a platter with cheese and crackers. "Are you hungry?" I asked.

"A little."

When I stepped back outside, the sun had set. I placed the platter on the ground and lit two citronella candles. Olivia slapped brie on one of the crackers.

"It's been a lot for you during the last few years. First your brother, and then Fiona."

I crumbled one of the crackers. Olivia was right. Sometimes I looked in the mirror and saw a person I hardly recognised. *I have become too serious. I wonder how would I know if my mental health starts slipping? Are my emotional*

CHAPTER 9

outbursts and my tiredness already signs that something is wrong? The call of a nearby owl interrupted my thoughts, but it didn't interrupt the chirping of the cicadas.

"You live in such a peaceful spot," Olivia said quietly.

"Yes," I sighed. "I love it here, I really do, but I might have to leave this place soon."

"What? Leave? You guys aren't thinking of selling the house?"

"No, Olivia. I'm looking for a house to buy for myself. I've made up my mind. I'm going to leave Tom."

I said what I had wanted to enunciate many times over the last six years. *There is never the perfect moment for a divorce,* I thought, and even now the moment wasn't perfect. Fiona wasn't fully recovered yet, and a separation might affect her badly. But I had tested the waters on our drive up north. I couldn't recall what exactly the topic had been, but Fiona had made a comment that had allowed me to prepare her.

"Dad doesn't ever listen to you," Fiona had said.

"I know."

"That's not right. You deserve to be with someone who listens to you."

"Yes, it's been like that for a long time. Unfortunately, I can't change your dad, or force him, so maybe I will not always be with him. Would you understand that?"

"Yes," she had replied steadily.

Olivia reacted in a similar way. Her tone was calm when she spoke. I knew that she would understand, unlike some of my other friends and my mother, who I expected to remind me of how hard-working Tom was, as if that were the only necessary prerequisite for a successful marriage.

"I've always thought you're so different from Tom, your views, and the way you are with the kids. You know what I mean," Olivia said, "but, tell me, did anything happen?"

"Not really. It's just that I've noticed how tense I am as soon as Tom comes into the house. His nervous energy drives me crazy."

"Yes, that's him. He can't relax."

"And there's so much more, as you know. The way he treats Eric, and blah,

blah, blah. At least once a month, he declares that Eric will grow out of his condition, like you can just grow out of autism. He wears me down with the logic, or I should say illogic, of his reasoning."

Olivia rested her feet against the wooden balustrade, leaned back in her chair, and gave me a sympathetic look.

"You're brave."

"Not really. I'm actually scared. Scared I'll get cancer or something like that. People get sick from mental stress. Tom rolls his eyes whenever I speak. I don't need this. He's not a friend anymore. I think the only thing that kept us together was our interest in travel and the kids. God knows, I might be doing him a favour, leaving."

"I don't think so. He adores you."

"Well, he doesn't show it," I said. "I need peace. Stillness. Nobody coming home at night. I just want to be by myself."

"What about Eric?"

"He'll move with me, of course."

"I guess he'll be glad."

"Sort of. You know, he doesn't like change. But you're right, he avoids Tom a lot. He'll be relieved in the end."

"He's such a sweet young man."

"Yes, I couldn't think of a better person to share a house with. He is a mellow guy, and he's quiet, or as Fiona puts it: It's not that he talks anyone's ear off."

Her description made us smile despite the seriousness of the topic.

After Olivia left that night, I thought intensely about Fiona. During the last few years, she had suffered from having an emotionally inaccessible father, just like I had suffered from having an emotionally unavailable husband. Both of us had secretly wished we could be the perfect family like the neighbours seem to be. The kind of family with the joking dad, the one with the bleached smile, who embraces his children, and kisses his wife on the cheeks. The kind you see in cereal advertisements on television. I knew that Tom would never fully understand my reasons for leaving him, but I was starting to feel okay with the idea. Sometimes two people just don't get each other and that's that.

CHAPTER 9

The day I signed an offer on a house less than an hour's drive from where we were living now, Vanessa called. She said that the girls had been fighting. She anticipated that Fiona would call me later in the evening. She also complained that the girls had not being doing their laundry and had left the kitchen messy after their late-night feasts. Her voice was tinged with anger. I felt uncomfortable.

When I apologised for my daughter's behaviour and promised a change, she sounded calmer.

I called Fiona and told her that I had just spoken with Vanessa, and that Vanessa seemed to be upset.

"Mum, I miss you," she said. She was trying to manipulate the conversation and deflect the issue.

"Miss you, too. Anyway, I've heard you had a fight with Sabrina."

"It's all good now, but Vanessa is so strict. She's not like you."

"I told you. Every household is different. But while you live with them, you have to play by their rules. Remember, Vanessa has four kids to look after. That's a lot. So, please, help out."

"I want to come home."

"Don't be silly. How's the eating going?"

"Good. Sally says that I'm doing really well."

A week later, I received another phone call from Vanessa. She was furious because the girls had gone out without telling her where they had gone. In fact, they had accepted a party invitation from a group of guys they had never met before. I was worried about Fiona making those unsafe and impulsive decisions, but I wasn't angry because I knew that I had pushed my luck worse than Fiona when I was younger.

Halfway through the night, Fiona had collapsed on the floor, and Brian had to go pick them up. She had been worried sick, Vanessa said. Fiona apparently recovered quickly and reassured everyone that her drink must have been spiked. The next morning, Vanessa had sat the girls down and read them the riot act.

Spiking drinks. Such an Auckland thing, Fiona texted me later, as if she were the local party expert now.

I began to wonder if she had fainted because she was eating too little.

During our next phone conversation, Fiona began to talk about panic attacks. She insisted on seeing Dr. Stevens during the upcoming Easter holidays. She needed medication to keep these attacks under control, she said.

I felt that it was time for her to come home. Sabrina's family needed a break, I wanted to get a clearer picture of what was going on with her, and I had to tell Fiona in person that Eric and I were moving out after Easter. Tom had been devastated when I had explained to him why I was leaving him, and surprised as if he had been blindfolded. He expressed a willingness to fix things, but for me, it was too late.

Eric didn't say much. He only asked pragmatic questions, such as: "How much longer will my commute to work be?" and "Can I have the largest bedroom in the new house?"

Fiona came home, and never returned to Auckland, for many reasons. Firstly, I decided that Brian and Vanessa shouldn't have to put up with her teenage craziness that had spiralled out of control.

"Can you get panic attacks from smoking weed?" she had asked Dr. Stevens with me in the room.

Jesus, I thought, *she's got asthma. I had told her not to smoke! Where did she get the damn weed from? Sabrina? Why was she smoking weed in a house where she was a guest? God knows what she had smoked to get panic attacks. And why did she drag me to the doctor to get pills for this?* Luckily, Dr. Stevens did not lose his cool. Whatever he thought of my parenting skills that day, he hid it well.

When I talked with Fiona about the weed, she said that Sabrina had gotten it from friends. She was afraid to smoke it again, because she thought it might make her anxious.

Another reason was that Fiona refused to fly back.

"Your parents will weigh you, when you get home," Brian had said to her jokingly one night after she had barely touched her dinner. "You won't be able to come back, if you don't eat."

CHAPTER 9

We were sitting on the steps that led up to our house, watching Winston chase the cat, when she told me about Brian's insensitive remark.

"It's hard, Mum," she sobbed, "because sometimes the family does make comments about big people. And when Laura sneaks chocolate bars out of the pantry, they tell her off, saying that she'll get fat."

"I guess that's how everyone talks these days. It's become part of our culture to judge fat people. It's almost as if being fat is worse than being mean. That's not to say that obesity isn't a problem. But guess who's to blame for that? The food and diet industries. Anyway, that's a discussion for another time. But honestly, I think that your condition has made you hypersensitive to comments about weight. My brain registers only half of what you hear."

"I still don't want to go back."

"And why is that?"

Fiona looked down at her bare feet. "You were right. I mean, I wanted to keep my promise and eat well, but then by being away from you, it was easy to restrict. I know it's wrong. I need to recover."

Although I hated having to call Vanessa and explain the situation, I had no other choice. The same day, I pressed the family-based therapy guidebook in Fiona's hands, and she began to feed herself.

As soon as she was back on track with her eating, Tom and I sat down with her at the kitchen table and told her about our separation in the gentlest way possible, if there is such a thing as speaking gently about splitting up a family. When she began to cry, I hoped that she cried because Tom did too, but I knew this wasn't the case. She was upset about me leaving the place that she called her home.

She decided to stay with her father because he lived closer to school, and because her caring personality would not allow her to leave him sad and alone.

"You'll have to self-manage, because Dad is at work all day," I said to her that night.

"I will."

"And if you run into problems, you can always come and stay with me, of course."

"But I want you to still come to the house," she pleaded.

"Poppy, that's ridiculous, I can't do that. I'll only live forty minutes away by car. You can come and see me any time, and I can also meet you in town after school, and remember, before you know it, you'll be at uni."

Initially Fiona chose to visit me every Wednesday after school. She would bring her homework, and while she read, wrote, and studied, I would prepare a nutritious dinner. She would eat well, and then she would spend the night in the room that I had set up for her. On one of those Wednesdays, Fiona told me that she adored her new class teacher, a man my age with a long, grey beard and a beaded necklace.

"He reads the news to us every morning. And he tells us not to believe everything we read, just like you do. You should meet him. You guys would have heaps to talk about. You would never stop yapping."

I laughed.

"He's been so supportive of me. I really like him."

I was glad. Diane, who was still her dean, also had given her a warm welcome-back hug, and she had tweaked Fiona's curriculum schedule so that her subjects matched the ones that she had taken in Auckland.

"Tony and I are friends now, but we're no longer going out. I finished with him for good."

First, I was baffled by the matter-of-fact tone in her voice, then I understood.

It seemed like everything in life was a process.

It must have been June when Fiona and I flew to Dunedin to participate in the open day program of the city's university, because I remember it being damp and ice cold. To make matters worse, I had booked a low-cost hotel. As soon as I saw the stack of woolly blankets on the beds, I knew that at night temperatures would be capable of taming even the most rebellious teenagers. The only thing the accommodation had going for it was that we could walk to the university campus where we'd be spending most of our time.

We attended zoology, German and global studies lectures, we inspected residential colleges and admired the historical buildings of New Zealand's oldest university. We also went clothes shopping, slurped chai lattes in between lectures, and dined in restaurants. Only when it was dark did we return, exhausted, to what we called "Our Ice Palace," switching on the electric heater to the highest setting possible and disappearing under layers of blankets.

On the last night, I sat on my bed trying to read through the prospectuses that we had collected throughout our stay, but I was too sleepy from the fresh air. I dropped the literature on the old-fashioned carpet and looked over at Fiona. She was already sound asleep under her pile of blankets.

It suddenly struck me how different this trip had been compared to our Christchurch trip one year ago. Unlike back then, Fiona displayed no rigidity around food anymore; she ordered different types of calorie-rich dishes without hesitation. In fact, she made pleasant conversation while we ate, and she confidently used the changing rooms in the clothes shops. I had to admit to myself that she had come such a long way since then.

With my eyes resting on the 1960s wallpaper that was peeling off in the corners of the room, I smiled. It was all too easy to stubbornly focus on the end of the recovery journey while what seemed like small improvements escaped one's peripheral vision.

In September, Fiona's face took on a greyish colour, and I noticed that she looked as if she was withering away. Concerned about her eating, I spoke to Tom, but he reassured me that she was eating a lot.

What he forgot to mention was that he was dating again and spending a lot of time away with his girlfriend, so he didn't really know what our daughter was doing.

It also hadn't escaped me that Fiona was cancelling numerous Wednesday visits, and when she did come, she rarely brought homework. She explained that she was busy because she had taken up a bar tendering job. But when she called in sick every other Sunday lunchtime, they let her go.

The weather improved, and I decided to spend a lazy afternoon with her at a smoothie bar with a beautiful garden. For hours, we sat on the grass under a blooming apple tree, engaged in deep conversation. Amongst many other things, Fiona told me that Anthony was going around badmouthing her. I wanted to embrace her, but she waved away my offer of comfort with a teaspoon, informing me that she had a new group of friends. Most of them were boys I knew. Tall skinny stoners with pimples and low self-esteem who, in their unchanging delirious state, forgot to eat. I wasn't keen on any of them, but I didn't say this to her. She told me that all of them would party in Eric's old apartment when Tom was away on the weekends.

I felt uneasy. "Just make sure they don't take advantage of you."

"They won't," she replied. "Don't worry."

My apprehension persisted when she started to visit me on Monday mornings instead of going to school. Apparently, she had already passed the year, and her interest in going to classes was shrinking. But I suspected that there was something else going on, because she would refuse desserts again and lie on my couch with a pillow over her head.

"Are you eating enough?" I would ask, with my stomach churning.

"Yes!" she would hiss at me.

"What is it, then?"

"There is no purpose to life. I just can't be happy anymore."

"Fiona, maybe you've lost track of your main goal, which is overcoming your eating disorder. Are you sure you are discussing *everything* that's bothering you with Sally? Your recovery is the most important thing in your life. What good is a university degree if you are still struggling with bulimia?"

Most of the time she would switch off while I was speaking and pretend she was sleeping. Even I was getting tired of having the same conversations over and over again. I wrote to Sally about these Monday morning low moods, saying that if the situation wouldn't change, there was no way Fiona would be ready to go to university.

Whatever Sally discussed with Fiona I didn't know, but when I met her the following week in town for lunch, she looked as if life had become brighter again.

Just as I thought Fiona's mood was improving, she called early in October to tell me that she had been awarded a scholarship worth thousands of dollars for overcoming hardship and achieving excellence in Year 12—but she sounded

CHAPTER 9

upset.

"Dad said, 'Oh, well, you're not even going to Otago,'" she sobbed. "Like he didn't even acknowledge it."

"For crying out loud! Does this man ever think before he speaks? A scholarship is a big deal, especially since a lot of students with eating disorders drop out of school." I was outraged. Who cared that in the meantime she had decided to study in Wellington.

"My friend Matt's parents said they are proud of me, and they aren't even my parents," she said, her voice shaky.

"Well, I know how difficult it was for you last year to attend school, let alone get Excellences. I am proud of you, Fiona. I think we should celebrate. Eric and I will take you out for dinner."

Then New Year's Eve came around. I was looking forward to a peaceful one without firecrackers, champagne, and people, but this all changed when Fiona came shooting up my driveway in Tom's car. I had just returned from a walk with Winston, and she nearly hit the poor animal because she wasn't looking.

Tears flooded down her face as she stepped out of the vehicle. "I need to talk."

"Let's go inside, make a cup of tea, and chat," I said trying to keep my voice steady. "I thought you were going to a party tonight?"

She shook her head. "Not anymore." She followed me into the kitchen.

I switched the kettle on.

"I'm addicted to Ecstasy."

"You're *what?*"

There was a long silence. I was careful not to burn my hands while pouring those two cups of tea that I knew we would never drink. *Those boys*, I thought, and in my head, I cursed them like a pirate.

"Don't tell Dad," Fiona whimpered.

"What the hell, Fiona? You have to explain yourself. I will *have* to tell your father, because you live with him. Where is he anyway?"

"He's with his girlfriend sorting things out, like, she's moving into the house next week."

Could he not have waited? Fiona will be at university in six weeks. As if it isn't hard enough for Fiona that I'm gone. But there was nothing to be gained anymore from being angry at him.

"What makes you think that you're addicted to Ecstasy?" I asked her.

"I started off taking it every other weekend, but now I want to take it more often and in higher dosages."

"Phew, that's no good." I sat down in the velvet armchair that I had taken with me when I moved out and remained silent for a while, unsure what to say next.

Fiona sat across from me on the sofa. She put her feet up on my knees and cuddled Winston who had leaped on the sofa.

"Why did you start taking it?"

"Initially the boys gave it to me for free. I wanted to party with them, but I didn't want to drink alcohol because it has too many calories. MDMA makes me feel good. I want to feel normal again, happy like everyone else."

"That's why I told you that recovery has to be a priority."

"I'm scared, Mum. I want to stop."

My voice was patient when I suggested that she should move in with me for the next three or four weeks. As far as I understood, the boys had partied with her every weekend in the apartment at Tom's. His daughter had been high on drugs right under his nose. In my opinion, Fiona needed to quit seeing these friends until she was off to uni. I offered to take her to the beach every day, to cook delicious food, and to lift her motivation. She didn't say anything for an hour or so, but then her mood flipped.

"I'm not staying. Not one night! " she yelled.

"How else do you think you're going to get over this Ecstasy shit?" I raised my voice.

"I'm not staying!"

"I thought you came here to sober up?!" I shouted. "You *are* staying!"

"You can't lock me up!" she screamed.

"I'm not locking you up, Fiona!" Panic tears swelled up in my eyes. I raised my voice even further and said that her suicidal thoughts after a weekend of being on drugs had scared me. I pleaded with her to accept my help.

CHAPTER 9

But instead, she got up, walked into her bedroom and threw the few clothes that she kept at my place into the little bag that she had brought.

"I hate your place! I'm going back to Dad's!" She yelled at the top of her lungs.

"Why, Fiona? Please, stay!" I was crying now.

"Stop guilt-tripping me!"

Paralysed, I watched her reverse the car out of the driveway. Then, very slowly, I closed the front door with both hands, walked into my room and shut the bedroom door. I sat down on my bed and watched my body tremble.

I never wanted to see her again.

Chapter 10

After months of mulling over what could be described as a failed marriage, I had begun to reclaim my life. The place I now called my home was freshly painted in off-whites and Mexican-inspired bright shades. Laminate flooring was installed throughout the house, and fruit trees were planted.

Day by day, I rediscovered premarital passions, which uplifted my spirits. I began to play tennis. I listened to music. I meditated. I studied. And I had plans to travel. My intention was that 2022 was going to be a good year, but after the New Year's Eve fallout with Fiona, I began to wonder how much influence I really had on life's events.

She had hurt me deeply by refusing my help. What was even worse was that Tom, after having had a mini pep talk with Fiona about the dangers of drugs, and several other people, who had heard about the situation through hearsay, rang to tell me how much Fiona was using me. I should cut her off all financial support, was their advice. She was buying drugs with my money. She should buckle up and get a job, that would stop her from not eating and getting into trouble, they said.

They predicted that she would drop out of university, because I had spoiled her. She was taking things for granted. She never had to fight or work for anything, they said.

Eric noticed how upset I was. He kept putting his heavy arm around my shoulders. Then, one Saturday evening, he offered to barbecue chicken thighs.

I lit the wood in the fire pit and set the outdoor table.

"I don't know what to think anymore," I said to him after we had finished eating. "All I know is that I don't want to see Fiona right now. I'm too upset about everything."

"You better hold your breath. I bet she'll come next week asking for money, or crying about something," he said in a staccato voice. "You'll never get rid of her."

"Eric!" I reprimanded him laughingly.

As usual he forgot to sift the bluntness from his statements.

"I don't want to get rid of her. It's just that I feel so used, and then again, I don't want to believe that she's intentionally taking advantage of me. I've always been her friend."

"You're not her friend." Eric shook his head. "You're her mother."

"You know what I mean."

"She doesn't have any friends," he said, "just like me, but I'm fine with it."

"You're not so wrong there. I wish she'd never told anyone about her bulimia. She told me that she feels she constantly has to live up to the expectations that come with the bulimic label. When everyone around you looks at you and thinks: bulimic, how do you create a new identity for yourself? It was Sally who animated her to tell people. I guess it's encouraged by therapists to reduce shame and societal stigma, or stuff like that, but it only elicited contempt. The girls in her class compared her with the other girls who they knew had eating disorders and told her that she didn't have it as bad. Teenagers are cruel. I've been around them for many years. I know."

"Yeah, they called me gay and stupid in school."

"Exactly. It's wishful thinking to assume that adolescents react with great understanding. Even if they did, there will always be the one who'll call the person with the eating disorder a drama queen. Most adults don't even understand eating disorders properly because they go so much deeper than dieting."

"I don't understand them." He squirted a bit of ketchup on the side of his plate and shook his head.

"It's because you love to eat," I chuckled. "Fiona used to love to eat too, but her brain doesn't allow her to enjoy the taste of food anymore. Eating doesn't calm her, instead it signals danger. It's something we cannot imagine."

My conversation with Eric prompted me to return to my study about eating disorders. Every night I read for an hour or so. I rarely came across new information. And yet, I had this feeling that I still didn't fully understand the bulimic mindset. Then one evening, I encountered an online talk by a psychiatrist who had studied eating disorders for over forty years. I decided to have a listen, leaned back onto my pillows, and turned up the volume.

A few minutes into her lecture, the psychiatrist switched on the walkie talkie that she was holding in her hand. While you could hear fuzzy words escaping from the device saying something about not eating, as well as disturbing hissing noises like that of a radio not accurately tuned into the station, she continued with her talk. But she had to raise her voice to speak over the noise. Then the noise grew louder, forcing the psychiatrist to further raise her voice. *Shut this thing off*, I thought annoyed. *I can't hear what you're saying.* But she didn't. She talked and talked and talked. Over the voice, over the hissing, and over the crackling. This is what her patients heard while they ate, she said.

Shameful tears rolled down my face. Why had it never crossed my mind that the noise in Fiona's head would be this tormenting, when all we had done for months was talk about that voice? Why had I never imagined it to be this distressing? Why did I need such an explicit demonstration to finally comprehend?

I rewound the video again and again, making sure that I would never forget how irritating and brutal the noise of this mental illness was. It was almost like a tinnitus barking orders at her, accusing her, and criticising her. A noise that had made it impossible for her to answer the waiter who had asked her what she would like to eat, or the teachers who had asked her about her work. That's why she would sit, absent-minded and in silence, while friends chatted. While I had sat with her. Sticking fingers in her ears to block out the noise and find some inner peace was futile.

If nothing else, she would pray for the volume to be at a bearable level, to be tolerable, but that only happened when she binged, threw up, exercised, didn't eat, or took drugs, I could hear her say.

Two weeks into the New Year, Fiona came to visit. I was taking an almond

CHAPTER 10

cake out of the oven when the front door opened, and she bounced into the house. I immediately noticed that she was well-rested, and her skin looked as if she had spent a few days at the beach.

"Smells good in here," she said as she threw her bag on the dining table and gave Winston a cuddle. "How have you been, Mum?"

"Lovely to see you, Fiona," I said. "Would you like a coffee and a piece of cake?"

"Yes, please," she replied.

She sat down on the wooden bench that matched the dining table and quietly watched me until I arrived with mugs and plates. I took a seat across from her and folded my hands.

She lowered her eyes and blew on her coffee before she apologised. "I want to make a fresh start," she said. "I've stopped taking drugs, and I'm cleaning myself up. I want to start ballet again, and I've already looked at classes. I'm going to take my studies seriously." She paused and looked up. "Actually, I can't wait to get to Wellington."

"That's really good of you, Fiona."

"I won't disappoint you."

"It isn't about disappointing *me*, darling. It's about you. About *you* overcoming the eating disorder. It's about you having to learn to cater for yourself. It's about you moving forward in life and being happy. Drugs will be in the way. And your eating disorder, too."

"I know," she said.

I reached for her hands. "Look, I don't care how well you'll do in your first year as long as you go to your classes and try. The only thing that worries me is that the halls are self-catering, so you'll have to talk with Sally about strategies for feeding yourself."

"Done already."

"Good. Well, I'm terribly sorry about New Year's Eve, Fiona. I didn't mean to shout. I understand that you're upset that Mum and Dad split up. But it isn't your fault. It's life. Relationships are tricky. For the last six years or so, I've tried to fix things, because I wanted to spare you the hurt, but I didn't succeed. Your dad is much happier now, and I am, too. His new girlfriend seems a good match. She's nice, you said?"

"Yes, she's nice to me, but he's already not listening to her."

"Oh, well, let's hope she doesn't notice," I said. And we smiled at each other. "If in any way I have hurt your feelings, again, I'm very sorry," I said. "I do understand your struggle. Sometimes it's just hard for me to accept that the recovery process is long and not linear. But I know you try hard. The reason why I sometimes overreact is because I love you so much. It's ironic, isn't it?"

"I love you, too," she said with a soft voice, and then she stood up, wrapped her arms around my neck and kissed my cheek. "You're the best."

The summer weeks passed quickly. Before we knew it, we sat squashed in my tiny car, surrounded by pillows, shoes, random bags and suitcases, plastic plants, a laptop, and a skateboard. We were about ten minutes into our trip to Wellington when we decided to sing along to Fiona's playlist. We got muddled up several times with the lyrics and burst out into explosive laughs with overflowing tears because it eased our nervousness. After we had made several trips back and forth from the car park to the student flat with the old shopping trolley that Fiona had found on the sidewalk, she set up her room while I walked back and forth in the apartment that she was going to share with five other students. None of them had arrived yet, which made it particularly hard for me to say goodbye to her.

She looked tiny and self-conscious in this empty flat, just like her plastic plant that sat lonely on one of the kitchen shelves. I stood briefly by the window trying to see the street from the fourth floor.

People throw themselves out of these tall city buildings, and their bodies splatter all over the pavement, shot through my head. *It happens.*

"Can I have a tea, before I go?" I asked her and turned away from the window. "I think I packed some."

"Sure, Mum," she replied. "I'll make you one."

"Good that you will still connect with Sally while you study."

"Yes, I know. By the way, have I told you that Dr. Stevens put me on this anti-anxiety medication for a wee while, because I'm a bit nervous about starting uni?"

"Oh, that's good. I hope it helps. You know, you can always call when things get complicated," I assured her.

She knew.

Fiona rang often. Usually around midnight, hoping that I would still be up. On occasion, she would ring me when she was at a party. She would make me speak to random people just for fun, or she would film her friends when they were drunk. I would smile because I could hear her cheeky laughter in the background.

Other times, she would call to talk about how much she liked her courses and her new life. We didn't avoid bulimia as a topic, but I left it up to her to bring it up. And she did, but not often.

Before I flew to Germany to visit my mother, I spent a day in Wellington and stopped by her halls. Fiona was proud to introduce me to her flatmates. She wrapped her arm around my waist while we walked around the city, and she showed me places that she had discovered and that were unknown to me. She wanted me to see that she was severing ties with the hair twisting and pleasing girl. She wanted me to be proud of her.

For lunch, we stopped at a sushi bar. Before Fiona sat down, she removed her fleece jacket and hung it over the back of her chair. She was wearing a singlet that now exposed her arms. Both were covered in bruises. I tried to ignore them, but while we talked and ate, I caught myself several times examining them. Each time, my stomach tightened. I didn't know what they were from, and I didn't ask. I didn't want to lift the thin layer of cheerfulness. She was so happy to see me, and I had missed her so much.

Later in the conversation, she mentioned that she had tried this horse tranquilliser drug, but it had freaked her out and she would never touch it again.

"Why would you swallow something that is clearly meant to be for animals?" I asked.

She pretended to look at me with contempt, but at the same time, she giggled, and I smiled to cover up my honest concern.

"This isn't funny, Fiona."

"I know. The floor was tilted for ages. It was horrible."

"Just don't do it again."

"I won't. I told you."

I left upset, thinking about her impulsiveness when it came to drugs. I thought about the bruises. *Was she harming herself?* Allowing Fiona to go to university suddenly felt like playing Russian roulette. I wasn't sure I had made the right decision by encouraging her to go.

In August I returned to the same retreat centre where I had sat two years and eight months ago. I arrived late afternoon. When I stepped out of my car, I threw my arms up in the air, and took a deep breath. In a few minutes, the sun would disappear behind the rolling hills that formed this untouched valley. I was happy to be back.

Along with the other twenty people who had turned up, I left my phone in the glove box. A small bag with loose-fitting clothes, toiletries, and my warm Ecuadorian blanket were all I carried into my spartan room with its single bed, desk, and chair. It was comforting to know that for the next week and a half, there would be no dramas and no emergencies, only teachings, meditation, nature walks, and delicious vegetarian food. Even talking was optional.

Back then, I had been so angry at the world. This time was different. I noticed it when, for reasons I don't remember, the tea break conversation turned to the topic of eating disorders. I mentioned that I had a daughter who was recovering from bulimia.

"You know," started the grey-haired woman who stood next to me, "the daughter of my neighbour, such a lovely family, well, I tell you, she's been diagnosed with bulimia or anorexia. It's all the same thing, isn't it? Anyway, I just don't get it, it seems to be such a pandemic these days. All the young people have it, even her, I mean, the neighbours are a lovely family. You wouldn't think you'll end up with something like that when you come from a good home. I really feel for the parents."

I nodded. By now I was used to hearing this stuff. My pride wasn't wounded anymore. I didn't feel the need to explain anything to her. There is a time and a place for everything, and I came here to connect with my inner self and not to educate people. I wanted to unwind and perhaps learn a few useful things to prepare myself for an unknown future, because there was always the possibility that Fiona wouldn't recover. That she'd relapse. Or worse.

My inner tension made me skip the early morning meditation for the first two days. I showered while everybody else was sitting on cushions in the freezing *gompa* steadying their minds. At lunch, I took more food than I needed, and I ate too fast. During the afternoon teachings, my legs fell asleep, and my knees began to ache. I felt a sharp pain shooting down my arm, reminding me that I had several herniated discs. *Perhaps I should have booked a beach retreat on Hawaii, where I could lie flat on the ground?* The teachings were complicated, and I began to wonder if philosophical concepts might be easier to understand in a horizontal position.

"Are you getting it?" I asked a white-haired man called Charles who sat across from me at the dinner table that evening. "I mean this talk about attachment. I'm not sure if I belong here."

He chewed and chuckled and chewed some more before he took the time to respond. "It's only Day Two, my dear," he said with his really deep voice.

"I know."

"Attachment is a difficult concept. It took me several years to understand it properly. Have a little patience with yourself." He smiled.

"I guess you're right."

"Patience is a virtue. Work on it," he insisted. Then he got up and asked me if he could get me a few scoops of apple crumble.

"Sure. I mean, yes, please. Thank you."

Neither Charles nor I said a word while we ate our dessert. For the first time since I had arrived, I slowed down to taste before I swallowed. I was glad that Charles's calm sucked all the nervous energy that I was emitting out of the air.

After we finished eating, I carried our dishes into the kitchen. I squeezed past chairs with people who were debating, sharing experiences, nodding, clearly enjoying each other's company. I opened the glass sliding door and stepped outside onto the deck. I slipped into my fur boots and threw my blanket over my shoulders. Because it was already dark outside, I had to use a flashlight to find and wind my way around flower beds and the occasional wet patch in the large grassy area that led to my room. Somebody had said that it was going to be a cold night with perhaps below-zero temperatures. Knowing that I would be too tired to set up my room after the evening teachings, I switched on the powerful electric heater and pulled my pyjamas out of the bag. I covered my sleeping bag with an additional blanket and walked over to the window to shut the curtains when the moving light of a distant torch caught my attention.

Curious, I peered outside. It was Charles circumambulating the white stupa with its majestic dome. I was sure he was on bare feet.

"Half the time, we're neurotic," our spiritual teacher said and smiled because she enjoyed provoking us. "It's because we can't cope when we don't get what we want."

And with that, the Ven. Rachel finished for the night. She closed her eyes.

I put my pencil down, placed both hands on my lap, right on left, palms facing upwards, the tips of my thumbs touching, and I also closed my eyes.

During these last years, a lot had happened that I had not wanted. The crisis that had unfolded around me had tensed the lines in my face. And the less gas I had left in my tank, the more obsessed I had become with my daughter's recovery. I had written far too many emails to Sally, often asking the wrong questions.

Every time I saw Fiona, I had checked her cheeks for signs of vomiting and checked her waistline in the hope that she had gained an ounce, before I listened to what *she* had to say. I had turned neurotic just like the nun had said—and stubborn, because I had wanted her recovery on my terms.

My mind had declared war on an eating disorder voice that wasn't even mine. Now I realised that I could only blame my own overinflated negative thoughts for my intense pain, not Fiona or anybody else. If I wanted to benefit Fiona and myself, I had to change *my* mind. I had to finally accept that relapse was an integral part of a slow and fragile recovery process. She needed time

CHAPTER 10

to find new pathways to cope with stress and time to mature. I had to trust her. With that thought I opened my eyes.

Calmly, I stared at the cloths that the nun had draped over her body and at the hole in her dark blue sock. I was relieved to be in her presence. I knew it was ridiculous, but it felt as if she were my guardian angel. She looked so incredibly still. I wanted to be like her. And just when I wondered if she would ever move again, she readjusted her robe and wished us a good night.

I walked past Charles, who was on his way to the stupa, as I searched the pockets of my trousers for the room key. Then I remembered that I didn't need one. Here we trusted each other.

On the last day of the retreat, I decided to circle the stupa myself. My legs needed exercising after so much sitting. I folded my arms and tucked my hands under my armpits. While I walked, my mind skipped back a few decades. Ever since I was a little girl, I had been attracted to the idea of fearlessness. If fearlessness were a profession, that's all I would have ever wanted to be. So, from an early age, I had practised being fearless. I had run away from home when I was seventeen, and I had travelled to dangerous and remote places with little money. I had enjoyed the challenge, and perhaps it was my youth that had made me believe that I had nothing to lose. Then fearlessness became a habit. Only after my brother died had I turned frightened and panicky.

Fiona's diagnosis felt like another loss. Dramatic and crazy thoughts began to torment me. I grew brittle.

"In a fearful state, we are of no use to others," we were told this morning.

Out of ignorance, I had confused love and compassion with fear and worry. I could understand this now, because for the last few days, we had done nothing else but dissect these emotions.

I walked one last time around the stupa, then I was ready to pack my car.

The first thing Fiona asked me over the phone when I called her after the retreat was, "Do you still have all your hair?"

I laughed. "Darling, it's not that I've become a nun all of a sudden."

"Well, tell me about your week."

"I'll be in Wellington in a few hours. Let's chat then."

We agreed to meet at the harbour. I enjoyed the waterfront atmosphere, especially on days when the sun and a lack of wind intensified the colours.

Fiona came running towards me as soon as she saw me. We embraced.

"How are you?" I asked her.

She told me that she was off her medication and that she hadn't felt the need to talk to Sally for a couple of months now. I knew, because Tom and I had been splitting the cost for her therapy, however, it was nice to hear it coming from her.

"And I'm not body checking anymore. That's huge for me! I was so obsessed with it. And I'm also eating really well. I'm not mentally restricting anymore, either. I'm trying to stay off my phone as much as I can. I deleted Snapchat. It's so toxic."

"That's wonderful," I said.

"I really like my life in the city."

"I liked living in the city when I was young."

We walked arm in arm, talking quietly.

"How about the voice?" I asked. "Do you still hear it a lot?"

"Not really," she said confidently. "There are weeks when I don't hear it all."

"I'm so happy for you!"

"Anyway, how's everything with *you*?" she wanted to know.

"I'm doing really well, Fiona. I met a lot of nice people in the last few days, and I've learned a lot. I'm grateful for how life has turned out. I left the retreat with a new purpose. I'm trying to rewire my mind, challenge old beliefs, and do things differently, just like you."

"It's hard work."

"It sure is." I asked her if she wanted to sit down somewhere to have a bite.

"Yes, I'm hungry. Let's get something."

We stopped at a burger place. We decided to sit outside.

Fiona picked up the menu. "You know, the eating disorder voice can be so smart," she said. "Every once in a while, it sneaks back in, but it isn't always obvious. It takes time to realise it."

She sounded like a mature version of her old self, the way she analysed what was going on for her in a logical way.

I placed my head in my hands and looked into her eyes. "The reason why the eating disorder voice is so smart is because you're such a clever girl. It's your own voice after all."

"I never thought of it like that," she responded and paused to contemplate what I had said. Then she smiled, almost relieved and added, "but, yes, it makes perfect sense."

After we had ordered burgers and fries, we spoke about mindfulness and self-compassion. Fiona shared some bits and pieces about herself and her friends.

"I still think sometimes that I'm not good enough," she said.

"We all do. But you must never believe it. You're a very precious young lady."

She smiled again and picked up her burger. "I think the spiritual stuff that you're talking about, Mum, it should be part of therapy."

"Maybe you're right," I said. "But it's not everyone's cup of tea."

I left Wellington content. Not only had the bruises on Fiona's arms vanished, but the glow in her eyes had returned.

During the Christmas holidays, Fiona came to stay with me. She was still doing well. A few weeks into the new semester, she called and talked about feeling depressed and not being able to get out of bed.

"I think I'm bipolar," she said.

By then I knew that the word 'relapse' was a difficult word to pronounce. I told her to go back to Sally. And she did. The trigger for the relapse had been her dieting flatmate, but with the help of a few sessions, Fiona was back on track.

Sally said that Fiona doesn't need to see her any longer. Since then, she has been managing on her own.

We still talk a lot on the phone and in person. We talk about repairing her relationship with her father. We talk about how to structure her life when it becomes too much. We talk about sitting out urges to binge, should they ever reoccur. We talk about eating well.

I have noticed that every time we have a conversation, she is stronger and less vulnerable to relapse. She tells me that on those rare occasions when the bulimia voice does resurface to whisper something into her ear, she lets it say what it needs to say, checks for the evidence of that thought, shrugs her shoulders ... and lets it go.

I value the deep connection between us. I am immensely proud of her. I call her my warrior. I trust her.

Since the end of winter, I start my day differently. Rather than having breakfast inside, I take a seat outside on my favourite rock. I place my coffee mug in the grass. I balance my cereal bowl on my lap. I soak in the changes of the seasons, with Winston by my feet, who patiently waits for the bits of granola that I purposely drop on the ground. Both of us enjoy the fresh air. I don't even mind the stormy days, because my brittleness has vanished, and my heart is flooded with warmth and gratitude. It has been a privilege to walk alongside my daughter on her recovery journey.

Only on rare occasions, do I look back to the very beginning and wonder what it was that had turned her despair into a silent illness instead of a scream that I could have heard.

About the Author

SELINA ELISON

Born in Germany, Selina Elison now lives in New Zealand. She has a master's degree in international relations from the University of Leeds, UK, and a postgraduate degree in education from the University of Bristol, UK.

When she is not in her office, she volunteers for NGOs (non-governmental non-profits) abroad.

Check out Selina's website for access to recommended resources.

You can connect with me on:
🌐 https://www.selinaelison.com